PLATO'S GORGIAS

**Benjamin Jowett's translation
adapted by
Albert A. Anderson**

The Theater of the Mind, Volume I

©1994 Agora Publications, Inc., Millis, MA 02054

AGORA PUBLICATIONS, INC.
17 Dean Street
Millis, MA 02054

3rd Printing 1996

Cover design by Donald Krueger

This is an unabridged adaptation of Benjamin Jowett's translation of Plato's dialogue as it appeared in the 1873 edition published by Scribner, Armstrong, and Company. Changes in the language have been made so that the dialogue flows more naturally in the contemporary American English idiom. Numbers in brackets are the universal Greek text pages.

To order a dramatized version of this dialogue on audio cassette (ISBN 1-887250-00-X) call or fax 508-376-1073.

Printed in the United States of America
ISBN 1-887250-01-8

GORGIAS

Characters

CALLICLES, SOCRATES, CHAEREPHON, GORGIAS, POLUS

Callicles: Socrates, it's smart to be late for a fight, but not for a feast. **[447]**

Socrates: Are we late for a feast?

Callicles: Yes, a delightful feast. Gorgias just made a splendid presentation.

Socrates: My friend Chaerephon here is to blame, Callicles. He kept us loitering in the Agora.[1]

Chaerephon: Never mind, Socrates. I'm the cause of the problem, so I'll fix it. Gorgias is a friend of mine, and I'll have him repeat the presentation.

Callicles: What's the matter, Chaerephon? Does Socrates want to hear Gorgias?

Chaerephon: Yes, Callicles, that's why we came.

Callicles: Well, then, let's go to my house. Gorgias is staying with me, and he'll perform for you there.

Socrates: Good, Callicles; but will he answer our questions? I want to hear him tell about what he teaches and about the nature of his art. He can save the presentation for another time.

Callicles: There's nothing like asking him, Socrates. Actually, that's part of his presentation. He was just saying that anyone in my house may ask him any question and he'll answer.

Socrates: I'm glad to hear that. Will you ask him, Chaerephon?

Chaerephon: What should I ask him?

Socrates: Ask him who he is.

Chaerephon: What do you mean?

Socrates: I mean the kind of question that he would answer by saying that he is a cobbler, if he were a maker of shoes. Do you understand?

Chaerephon: I understand, and I'll ask him. Tell me, Gorgias, is what Callicles says true, that you will answer any question?

Gorgias: Quite true, Chaerephon, but it has been many years since anyone has asked me a **[448]** new question.

Chaerephon: Then you must be well prepared, Gorgias.

Gorgias: Go ahead and try me, Chaerephon.

Polus: If you like, Chaerephon, you may try me instead. Gorgias has been talking for a long time. I think he's probably tired.

Chaerephon: Polus, do you think you can answer better than Gorgias?

Polus: What difference does it make as long as it's good enough for you?

Chaerephon: No difference. So, go ahead and answer.

Polus: Go ahead and ask.

Chaerephon: Here's my question: If Gorgias had the skill of his brother Herodicus, what should we call him? Shouldn't the name be the same as the one given to his brother?

Polus: Certainly.

Chaerephon: Then it would be right to call him a physician?

Polus: Yes.

Chaerephon: And if he had the skill of Aristophon, the son of Aglaophon, or his brother Polygnotus, what should we call him?

Polus: Obviously, a painter.

Chaerephon: Now what should we call Gorgias; what is the art in which he is skilled?

Polus: Chaerephon, there are many human arts that are experimental and have their origin in experience. Experience allows human life to proceed according to art, and inexperience according to chance. Different people are proficient in different arts in different ways. The best people are proficient in the best arts. Our friend Gorgias is one of the best, and the art in which he's proficient is the noblest.

Socrates: Polus has learned to make a fine speech, Gorgias, but he's not keeping the promise he made to Chaerephon.

Gorgias: What do you mean, Socrates?

Socrates: I mean he hasn't answered the question.

Gorgias: Then ask him yourself.

Socrates: I would rather ask you. I can see from the few words Polus has spoken that he has paid more attention to rhetoric than to dialectic.

Polus: Why do you say that, Socrates?

Socrates: Because, Polus, when Chaerephon asked you about the art which Gorgias knows, you praised it as if you were answering someone who found fault with it. But you never said what the art is.

Polus: Didn't I say that it is the finest of the arts?

Socrates: Yes, but that's no answer to the question. Nobody asked about the quality. The question is about the nature of the art and about what we ought to call Gorgias. Please tell me in the same short and excellent way you answered

Chaerephon when he first asked you **[449]** about this art and about what we should call Gorgias. Rather, let me turn to you, Gorgias, and ask the same question. What is your art?

Gorgias: Rhetoric, Socrates.

Socrates: Then am I to call you a rhetorician?

Gorgias: Yes, Socrates, and a good one too, if you want to call me what "I boast to be," as Homer would put it.

Socrates: I do.

Gorgias: Then please do so.

Socrates: Can we also say that you make other men into rhetoricians?

Gorgias: Yes, that's exactly what I do, and not only in Athens.

Socrates: Will you continue to ask and answer questions, Gorgias, as we are doing now, and save for later the longer form of speech that Polus was attempting? Will you keep your promise and give only short answers to the questions asked?

Gorgias: Socrates, some answers are necessarily longer, but I will do my best to make them as short as I can. Part of my profession is that I can be as short as anyone.

Socrates: That's what I want, Gorgias; show us the shorter method now and the longer one later.

Gorgias: I will, and I'm sure you'll praise the unrivaled brevity of my speech.

Socrates: You say that you're a rhetorician and a teacher of rhetoricians. What's the business of rhetoric? Is the business of weaving making garments?

Gorgias: Yes.

Socrates: Is the business of music the composition of melodies?

Gorgias: Yes.

Socrates: Gorgias, I do admire the brevity of your answers!

Gorgias: Yes, Socrates, I think I'm good at that.

Socrates: I'm glad to hear it. Now answer in the same way about rhetoric. What's the business of rhetoric?

Gorgias: Discourse.

Socrates: What sort of discourse, Gorgias? The kind that would tell sick people what treatment would make them well?

Gorgias: No.

Socrates: Then rhetoric doesn't deal with all kinds of discourse?

Gorgias: Certainly not.

Socrates: Yet rhetoric does enable people to speak?

Gorgias: Yes.

Socrates: And to understand what they're talking about?

Gorgias: To be sure.

Socrates: Doesn't the art of medicine enable people to understand and talk about the sick? **[450]**

Gorgias: Certainly.

Socrates: Then medicine also deals with discourse.

Gorgias: Yes.

Socrates: With discourse concerning diseases?

Gorgias: Certainly.

Socrates: Doesn't gymnastics also deal with discourse concerning the good or bad condition of the body?

Gorgias: Very true.

Socrates: Gorgias, the same is true of all the other arts; all of them deal with discourse concerning their subject matter.

Gorgias: That is evident.

Socrates: Then if you call rhetoric the art that deals with discourse, and if all of the other arts deal with discourse, why don't you call all of them arts of rhetoric?

Gorgias: Because, Socrates, knowledge of the other arts deals only with some kind of external activity involving the hands; but there is no such activity involving the hands in rhetoric. It operates and produces its effect in the medium of discourse. Therefore, it is correct to say that rhetoric deals with discourse.

Socrates: I'm not sure I understand what you're saying, but I intend to find out. Please answer this question: Would you say that arts do exist?

Gorgias: Yes.

Socrates: In some of the arts a lot is done but little or nothing is said. In painting, sculpture, and many other arts the work takes place in silence. Would you say that these are arts with which rhetoric has no concern?

Gorgias: You understand my meaning perfectly, Socrates.

Socrates: There are other arts that work only with words and involve little or no action—for example, arithmetic, calculation, geometry, and playing checkers. In some of these, words are nearly identical with the things, but in most of them, words predominate over things. Their effectiveness and power come from words. Do you mean that rhetoric is this kind of art?

Gorgias: Exactly.

Socrates: I don't think that you really mean to call these arts rhetoric, but the precise expression you used was that rhetoric is an art which produces its effect through the medium of discourse. An adversary who wished to be critical might say: "So, Gorgias, you call arithmetic rhetoric."

I don't think that you would call arithmetic rhetoric any more than you would call geometry rhetoric.

Gorgias: You are quite right, Socrates. **[451]**

Socrates: Well, then, let me have the rest of my answer. Given that rhetoric is one of the arts which works mainly by the use of words and that there are other arts which also use words, tell me the quality of words by which rhetoric has its effect. Suppose a man were to ask me about any of the arts I mentioned just now. He might say: "Socrates, what is arithmetic?" If I were to reply, as you did just now, that arithmetic is an art which produces an effect by words, then he might ask: "Words about what?" I would say: "Words about odd and even numbers and how many there are of each." And what if he asked again: "What is the art of calculation?" I would say: "That also is one of the arts which work entirely by using words." But then he might again ask: "Words about what?" I would then say that it's similar to arithmetic, but with a difference. The difference is that the art of calculation considers the quantities of odd and even numbers both in relation to each other and in and of themselves. Now suppose I said astronomy also works entirely by words. He would ask: "Words about what, Socrates?" I would answer that the words of astronomy are about the motions of the sun, the moon, and the stars and their relative speed.

Gorgias: Very true, Socrates. I admit that.

Socrates: Now, let's have from you, Gorgias, the truth about rhetoric. You would admit, wouldn't you, that it's an art which operates and produces all of its effects through the medium of words?

Gorgias: True.

Socrates: Tell me, what are the words about? To which class do the words that rhetoric uses belong?

Gorgias: To the greatest, Socrates, and to the best human things.

Socrates: That's ambiguous, Gorgias. I'm still in the dark. What are the greatest and best human things? I suppose you have heard the old drinking song in which the singers enumerate the goods of life: first health, then beauty, and third, as the poet says, wealth honestly obtained.

Gorgias: Yes, I know the song; but what is your point? **[452]**

Socrates: I mean that the producers of the things the song praises—the physician, the trainer, and the business person—will immediately challenge you. First the physician will say: "Socrates, Gorgias is deceiving you, because it is my art, not his, which produces the greatest good." And when I ask who he is to say this, he'll answer: "I'm a physician." "What do you mean?" I'll say. "Do you mean that your art produces the greatest good?" Then he'll say: "Certainly, for isn't health the greatest good? What greater good can men have, Socrates?" Then the trainer will come and say: "Socrates, I'll be surprised if Gorgias can show that his art does more good than mine." I'll ask him who he is to say this, and he'll reply: "I'm a trainer, and my job is to make people beautiful and physically strong." As soon as I've finished with the trainer, the business person will arrive and will look down on all of them. "Socrates," the business person will say, "consider whether Gorgias or anyone else can produce any greater good than wealth." You and I will ask: "Are you a creator of wealth?" The business person will say "yes." We will ask: "Do you consider wealth to be the greatest good?" And the answer will be: "Yes, of course." But then I'll say: "My friend Gorgias contends that his art produces a greater good than yours," and the business person will surely ask: "What is this good?" Now, Gorgias,

I want you to answer this question: What is the good that you create?

Gorgias: Socrates, it really is the greatest good; it is what gives freedom to individuals and gives rulers the power of ruling over others.

Socrates: And what do you think that is?

Gorgias: It is the power of words that persuades judges in court, senators in the legislature, citizens in the assembly, or participants in any other public meeting. If you have this power, the physician and trainer will serve you. Because of your ability to speak and persuade others, the business person will make money for you.

Socrates: Now, Gorgias, I think you've accurately explained your understanding of the art of rhetoric. You say that rhetoric produces persuasion. This and nothing else is the summit and **[453]** goal of rhetoric. Do you know any effect of rhetoric greater than that of producing persuasion?

Gorgias: No, this definition seems fair, Socrates. Persuasion is the high point of rhetoric.

Socrates: Then listen to me, Gorgias. If there ever was a person eager to enter a discussion simply to know the truth, I'm such a person. I think you're another.

Gorgias: What are you trying to say, Socrates?

Socrates: I'll explain. I don't know what, according to you, is the exact nature of persuasion produced by rhetoric. Nor do I know its topics. But I do have a hunch about both. I'm going to ask you about the power of persuasion given by rhetoric and about its topics. But why, if I have a hunch, don't I simply tell you? It's not for your sake but to allow the argument to proceed in a way that is most likely to yield the truth. See if I'm right in asking this next question. Suppose I ask you: "What kind of painter is Zeuxis?" Then, if you tell me that he is a painter of figures, would I be justified in asking about the kind of figures and where we can find them?

Gorgias: Certainly.

Socrates: And the reason for asking this second question is that there are other painters who paint other kinds of figures?

Gorgias: True.

Socrates: But if no one but Zeuxis painted figures, then you would have answered well?

Gorgias: Certainly.

Socrates: Now I'd like to ask about rhetoric in the same way. Is rhetoric the only art that brings persuasion, or do other arts do it as well? For example, does a person who teaches persuade or not?

Gorgias: The person who teaches persuades, Socrates. There's no mistake about that.

Socrates: Let's consider the arts that we were talking about just now; do arithmetic and mathematicians teach us the properties of number?

Gorgias: Certainly.

Socrates: Therefore, they persuade us?

Gorgias: Yes.

Socrates: Then both arithmetic and rhetoric produce persuasion.

Gorgias: Clearly.

Socrates: If anyone asks what kind of persuasion and about what, we'll answer that it's the kind that teaches about the quantity of odd and even. Then we'll be able to show that all the **[454]** other arts we were just discussing produce persuasion, and we can explain what kind of persuasion and about what.

Gorgias: Quite true.

Socrates: So, rhetoric is not the only producer of persuasion?

Gorgias: True.

Socrates: Given that not only rhetoric produces persuasion but that other arts do as well, we might rightly pose a question similar to the one about the painter. What kind of persuasion does rhetoric produce and about what? Is that a fair way to put the question?

Gorgias: I think it is.

Socrates: Then, if you approve the question, Gorgias, what's the answer?

Gorgias: Socrates, rhetoric is the art of persuasion in courts and other assemblies, as I was just saying. And it's about the just and the unjust.

Socrates: That was my hunch, Gorgias. Now don't be surprised if later on I repeat what seems to be a simple question. As I said, I'm asking you not for your sake but for the sake of logical argument. I'm trying to avoid the habit of anticipating and speculating about the meaning of each other's words. I want you to be able to proceed in your own way.

Gorgias: I think that you are quite right, Socrates.

Socrates: Then let me ask this question. Is there such a thing as learning?

Gorgias: Yes.

Socrates: And there is also such a thing as believing?

Gorgias: Yes.

Socrates: Are learning and believing the same thing?

Gorgias: In my judgment, Socrates, they are not the same.

Socrates: Your judgment is correct, Gorgias, which you can demonstrate this way. If a person were to ask you whether there is false belief as well as true belief, I think you would reply that there is.

Gorgias: Yes.

Socrates: But is there false knowledge as well as true knowledge?

Gorgias: No.

Socrates: No, indeed! So, this proves that knowledge is different from belief.

Gorgias: That is true.

Socrates: But both those who have learned as well as those who have believed are persuaded?

Gorgias: That is as you say.

Socrates: Then should we assume two kinds of persuasion, one that is the source of belief without knowledge and the other the source of knowledge?

Gorgias: Yes.

Socrates: Which kind of persuasion about justice and injustice does rhetoric create in courts of law and other assemblies? Is it the kind of persuasion that gives belief without knowledge or the kind that gives knowledge?

Gorgias: Clearly, Socrates, it is that which only gives belief. **[455]**

Socrates: Then it would seem that rhetoric produces a kind of persuasion that creates belief about justice and injustice but does not teach about them.

Gorgias: True.

Socrates: And the rhetorician does not teach courts of law or other assemblies about justice and injustice but only creates belief about them? Surely nobody can teach so many people about such matters in a short time.

Gorgias: Certainly not.

Socrates: O.K., then let's see what we really mean about rhetoric, because I don't yet know what to think. When an assembly meets to select a physician, a shipbuilder, or any other skilled expert, will the rhetorician be consulted? I don't think so. In every selection the one who has the greatest skill ought to be chosen. It's the architect who should advise about the building of walls, harbors, and docks, not the rhetorician. When generals have to be chosen and a battle plan developed, then the military should advise, not rhetoricians. Don't you agree, Gorgias? You claim to be a rhetorician as well as a teacher of rhetoricians, so it would be best to learn the nature of your art from you. Let me assure you that I have your interest in mind as well as my own. It's likely that one or more of these young men here would like to become your student. In fact, I see several who have this desire, but they are too shy to question you. So, when you are questioned by me, please imagine that you are being questioned by them. "What's the point of coming to you, Gorgias," they will ask. "What will you teach us to advise the state? Will it only be about justice and injustice or also about the other things which Socrates just mentioned?" How will you answer them?

Gorgias: I like your way of leading the conversation, Socrates. I'll try to reveal to you the whole nature of rhetoric. I'm sure you've heard that the plans for the docks and walls of Athens, and for the harbor, were developed with advice from both Themistocles and Pericles, not at the suggestion of the builders.

Socrates: Yes, Gorgias, that's what they say about
Themistocles, and I personally heard Pericles' speech when
he advised us about the middle wall.

Gorgias: Notice, Socrates, that when a decision has to be
made in such matters, it's the rhetoricians who are the
advisers; because they are people who win arguments.
[456]

Socrates: That's what I had in mind, Gorgias, when I asked
about the nature of rhetoric. When I think about rhetoric in
this way, it always appears to me to be something
miraculous.

Gorgias: Miraculous, indeed, Socrates. If you only knew
how rhetoric embraces and holds all the inferior arts under its
power. I'll give you a striking example of this. Several
times I have been with my brother Herodicus or some other
physician to see a patient who would not take medicine or
agree to surgery. Through the use of rhetoric, I've persuaded
patients to do what the physician couldn't get them to do. If
a rhetorician and a physician were to go to any city and argue
before the assembly concerning who should be selected, the
physician would have no chance. The person who can speak
best will be selected in competition with anyone from any
other profession. The rhetorician can speak persuasively to
people on any subject. This is the miraculous power of
rhetoric, Socrates. However, rhetoric should be used selec-
tively, like any other competitive art. The rhetorician should
not misuse strength any more than a boxer, a wrestler, or
someone proficient in the other martial arts. The rhetorician
has powers that are superior both to friends and enemies, but
that doesn't provide a right to strike, stab, or slay other
people. Suppose a man who has been trained as a boxer
attacks his father, mother, or friend. That's no reason to
detest   trainers or to banish them from the city. They taught

their art for a good purpose, to be used against enemies and wrongdoers, in self-defense, not in aggression. Others have perverted their training, wrongly using their strength **[457]** and skill. There is nothing wrong with the teachers, nor is their art at fault or bad in itself. It is those who wrongly use the art who are to blame. The same is true of rhetoric. The rhetorician can speak against anyone on any subject, and he can usually persuade better than any other person. But it would be wrong for the rhetorician to destroy the reputation of a physician or any other professional merely as an exercise of power. Rhetoric ought to be used fairly, as in the case of martial arts. If someone becomes a rhetorician and then makes bad use of the art, that's no reason to detest the teachers or to banish them. The teacher intended that the student should make good use of what has been learned, not abuse it. Therefore, it is the student who should be detested, banished or put to death, not the teacher.

Socrates: Gorgias, you and I have had a lot of experience with argumentation. You must have observed that it doesn't always end by satisfying or educating the participants. Disagreements are likely to take place, and one person will often deny that what the other says is true or clear. When that happens, they stop reasoning and begin to quarrel, each imagining that the other person is speaking only from personal feelings. Sometimes they will go on attacking each other until their listeners become annoyed at their own tolerance in listening to them. Why do I bring this up? Because I can't help thinking that what you are saying now is inconsistent with what you first said about rhetoric. But I hesitate to point this out. I'm afraid you might think I'm hostile toward you and that I only speak from personal feeling rather than to discover the truth. But if you're the kind of person I am, I'd like to ask you some more questions. If not, then I'll leave you alone. What kind of person am I? I'm **[458]** one who is willing to be corrected if I say anything that's not true, and willing to correct anyone else who says what is untrue. I'm just as ready to be corrected as to correct, because I think it is even more beneficial—for the same reason it's better to be cured than to cure someone else. There's nothing worse than having a false opinion about the matters we're discussing. So, if you're the kind of person I am, let's continue the discussion, but if you would rather not, that's fine; let's quit.

Gorgias: Socrates, I am the kind of man you indicate, but perhaps we should consider our audience. Before you came, I had already made a long presentation, so if we continue, the argument may go on too long. Perhaps we should consider whether we are detaining people who would rather be doing something else.

Chaerephon: Gorgias and Socrates, I can speak for everyone here. We all want to listen to you. As far as I'm concerned, I can't imagine any business so important that would take me away from such an interesting discussion.

Callicles: Chaerephon, I've been present at many discussions, but I swear I was never more delighted than by this one. I'd be pleased to have you go on all day.

Socrates: Callicles, I'm willing if Gorgias is.

Gorgias: After all this, how could I refuse, especially in light of my offer to answer any question? Socrates, you begin; ask me any question you like.

Socrates: Then I'll tell you, Gorgias, what concerns me about what you've said, though perhaps you're right and I've misunderstood you. You claim that you can teach anyone who becomes your student to be a rhetorician?

Gorgias: Yes.

Socrates: And you will teach how to convince people on any subject, not by educating them but by persuading them?

Gorgias: Certainly. **[459]**

Socrates: In fact, you said that the rhetorician is more persuasive than the physician, even on medical subjects?

Gorgias: Yes, with the public.

Socrates: In other words, with ignorant people. To those who know, the rhetorician cannot be more persuasive than the physician.

Gorgias: True.

Socrates: In order to be more persuasive than the physician, the rhetorician must have greater persuasive power than the person who knows?

Gorgias: Certainly.

Socrates: Without being a physician?

Gorgias: Correct.

Socrates: Any person who is not a physician is ignorant of what the physician knows?

Gorgias: Clearly.

Socrates: So, when the rhetorician is more persuasive than the physician, the ignorant person is more persuasive with ignorant people than is the person who knows? Doesn't that follow?

Gorgias: In this case, yes.

Socrates: And rhetoric has the same relation to all the other arts. The rhetorician doesn't have to know the subject matter of those arts but only how to persuade ignorant people that the rhetorician has more knowledge than those who know.

Gorgias: Yes, Socrates. Doesn't that make things a lot easier? This way you only need to learn the art of rhetoric, and you can be as good as professionals who have learned the other arts.

Socrates: Whether the rhetorician is as good as the others remains to be seen, but we'll pursue that question when it's appropriate. I'd rather begin by asking whether the rhetorician is as ignorant of what is just and unjust, honorable and dishonorable, good and bad as of medicine and the other arts. I mean, does the rhetorician know the truth about these ideas or only know how to persuade ignorant people? Or is it necessary for the student to know these things before coming to you to learn the art of rhetoric? If the student is ignorant, you, the teacher of rhetoric, might refuse to teach these things, because that's not your business. You will, however, help the student pretend to the public to have such knowledge, even though it isn't true, and pretend to be a good person, even though that isn't true. Or, will you be **[460]** unable to teach rhetoric unless the student already knows these things? What do you say about this, Gorgias? Please explain the power of rhetoric as you promised.

Gorgias: Socrates, I suppose that the student who doesn't happen to know these things will have to learn them from me.

Socrates: That's right, Gorgias. So, the rhetoricians you train must know what is just and unjust, either by previous learning or by your teaching.

Gorgias: Certainly.

Socrates: Now, is a person who has learned woodworking a carpenter?

Gorgias: Yes.

Socrates: And the person who has learned music is a musician?

Gorgias: Yes.

Socrates: Similarly, one who has learned medicine is a physician? In general, when you learn any subject matter you are what your knowledge makes you.

Gorgias: That's right.

Socrates: By the same reasoning, a person who has learned the nature of justice is just?

Gorgias: Yes.

Socrates: And one who is just can be expected to do what is right?

Gorgias: Apparently.

Socrates: So, the rhetorician will be just, and therefore will desire to do what's right?

Gorgias: That clearly follows.

Socrates: Then the just person will never be willing to do wrong?

Gorgias: That is certain.

Socrates: And, according to the argument, the rhetorician will be just?

Gorgias: Yes.

Socrates: And therefore will never be willing to do what's wrong?

Gorgias: That's right.

Socrates: But do you remember saying that the trainer is not to be detested or banished if the boxer makes bad use of his training? Similarly, if the rhetorician makes a bad and unjust use of rhetoric, that is not to discredit the teacher, nor is the teacher to be blamed, but the wrongdoer who made bad use of rhetoric is to be blamed. Didn't you say that?

Gorgias: Yes, I did.

Socrates: But now it turns out that the student of rhetoric cannot have done what is wrong.

Gorgias: True.

Socrates: When we started talking, Gorgias, you said that rhetoric deals with discourse, not about odd and even, but about justice and injustice. Isn't that so?

Gorgias: Yes.

Socrates: When I heard you say that, I thought that rhetoric, which is always discussing justice, couldn't possibly be unjust. But then you said that the student of rhetoric might make bad use of rhetoric, and I was surprised by your inconsistency. Now we have agreed that the rhetorician is incapable of making unjust use of rhetoric or of willing what is unjust. **[461]** Gorgias, it's going to take a lot more discussion before we get to the truth of all this!

Polus: Socrates, do you really believe what you're saying about rhetoric? Simply because Gorgias was ashamed to deny that the rhetorician knows what's just, honorable, and good and can teach them to any ignorant person who comes along, you use your favorite mode of interrogation to accuse Gorgias of contradiction. Do you really think that anyone will ever admit not to know, or not to be able to teach, the nature of justice? The truth is that you are rude in leading the argument in this direction.

Socrates: Polus, the primary reason for having friends and children is that when we get old and stumble, a younger generation may be at hand to put us back on our feet, both in our words and in our actions. If Gorgias and I are stumbling, you are present to help us, as you should. Speaking for myself, I take back any error into which you think I may have fallen, but upon one condition.

Polus: What's that?

Socrates: That you shorten those long speeches you used at first.

Polus: What? Do you mean that I'm not free to use as many words as I please?

Socrates: My friend, I know it's hard to imagine that you have come to visit Athens, where speech is more free than in any other Hellenic state, and that you of all people might be deprived of the power to speak. But consider my case. Would I not be abused if, when you make a long oration and refuse to answer a question you are asked, I'm prevented from leaving and must stay and listen to you? On the contrary, if you're really interested in the **[462]** argument, or, to repeat what I said before, if you have any desire to help us back to our feet, then you are welcome to take back anything you please. On your part, you should ask and answer as Gorgias and I do—refute and be refuted. I suppose that you claim to know what Gorgias knows?

Polus: Yes.

Socrates: You, like Gorgias, invite anyone to ask you about anything and you know how to answer?

Polus: Certainly.

Socrates: Now, which would you like to do, ask or answer?

Polus: I will ask, and you, Socrates, will answer the same question you think Gorgias is unable to answer: What is rhetoric?

Socrates: Do you mean what kind of art?

Polus: Yes.

Socrates: If you want the truth, Polus, in my opinion it's not an art at all.

Polus: Then what, in your opinion, is rhetoric?

Socrates: In a paper of yours I recently read, it's something from which you claim to have created art.

Polus: What thing?

Socrates: I would call it a kind of experience.

Polus: Then you think rhetoric is a kind of experience?

Socrates: That's my view, if it's yours.

Polus: An experience of what?

Socrates: An experience of producing a kind of pleasure and gratification.

Polus: If it's able to gratify people, then wouldn't rhetoric be a fine thing?

Socrates: What are you saying, Polus? Why are you asking me whether or not rhetoric is a fine thing when I haven't yet told you what rhetoric is?

Polus: Didn't you tell me that rhetoric is a kind of experience?

Socrates: Because you are so fond of gratifying others, will you gratify me in one small matter?

Polus: I will.

Socrates: Will you ask me, what kind of art is making pastry?

Polus: What kind of art is making pastry?

Socrates: It's not an art at all, Polus.

Polus: What is it, then?

Socrates: I would call it a kind of experience.

Polus: Experience of what?

Socrates: Experience of producing a kind of pleasure and gratification.

Polus: Then are making pastry and rhetoric the same?

Socrates: No, they are only different parts of the same profession.

Polus: And what's that?

Socrates: I'm afraid that the truth may seem discourteous. I don't want Gorgias to imagine that I'm ridiculing his profession, so I hesitate to answer. Whether or not this is the art of rhetoric which Gorgias practices I really don't know. Based on what he was just saying, it **[463]** isn't clear exactly what he considers his art to be, but the rhetoric I have in mind is part of something that's not very nice.

Gorgias: A part of what, Socrates? Never mind me; say what you mean.

Socrates: To me, Gorgias, rhetoric is part of a practice created not by art but by the habit of a bold and clever mind, which knows how to act in the eyes of the world. I would call it flattery. This practice has several other parts, one of which is making pastry, which may seem to be an art, but isn't; it's only experience and routine. Another part is rhetoric; cosmetology and sophistry are the other two. So, there are four branches and four different things related to them. If he likes, Polus may ask me what part of flattery is rhetoric. I haven't told him yet. He didn't notice that I hadn't answered him about the nature of rhetoric when he proceeded to ask whether I think rhetoric is a fine thing. But I refused to tell him whether rhetoric is a fine thing until we have first determined the nature of rhetoric. That wouldn't be right, would it, Polus? But I'll be happy to answer the following question: "What part of flattery is rhetoric?"

Polus: What part of flattery is rhetoric?

Socrates: Let's see if you understand my answer. Rhetoric is the shadow of a part of politics.

Polus: Is that good or bad?

Socrates: I'd call it bad, though I'm not sure you understand what I'm talking about.

Gorgias: Socrates, I don't think I understand myself.

Socrates: That's not surprising, because I haven't yet explained what I mean. Our friend Polus, like the young colt he is, is likely to run away.

Gorgias: Never mind him. Explain to me what you mean by saying that rhetoric is the shadow of a part of politics.

Socrates: I'll try to explain my notion of rhetoric, and if I'm mistaken, my friend Polus will refute me. Is it correct to say that there are both bodies and souls? **[464]**

Gorgias: There are.

Socrates: Wouldn't you say that there's a good condition for each of them?

Gorgias: Yes.

Socrates: This condition, might it only appear good rather than really be good? I mean, there are many people who appear to be healthy, and only a physician or a trainer would see that they are not healthy.

Gorgias: True.

Socrates: You agree that this applies not only to the body but also to the soul? Either one may give the appearance of health but not really be so?

Gorgias: Yes, certainly.

Socrates: Now I'll try to explain what I mean. Since the body and soul are two in number, they have two arts corresponding to them. There is the art of politics, which tends the soul, and another art which tends the body, for which I don't know a specific name but which itself has two divisions, one called gymnastics and the other medicine. In politics, there are also two divisions: a legislative part, which corresponds to gymnastics, and justice, which corresponds to medicine. These two overlap, justice having to do with the same subject as legislation, and medicine with the same subject as gymnastics. But there is a difference between them. Now, seeing that there are these four arts which minister to the body and the soul for their highest good, flattery, which knows—no, guesses at—their nature, distributes herself into four imitations of them. It adopts the likenesses of one or another, pretending to be what it imitates, having no regard for people's best interest. It uses pleasure as bait for gullible people, deceiving them into believing that it is of the highest value to them. Pastry making disguises itself as medicine, pretending to know what food is good for the body. If a physician and a pastry maker entered a contest in which children (or men with no more sense than children) were the judges concerning which of them best understands the goodness or badness of food, the physician would starve to death. Polus, now I'm talking to you. I call this flattery, and I think it's a bad thing, because it aims at pleasure instead of goodness. I **[465]** don't call it art but only experience and routine, because it's unable to give a reason for the nature of its uses. I don't call anything irrational an art. If you question my words, I'm prepared to argue in their defense.

Making pastry, then, is the kind of flattery which impersonates medicine, and cosmetology impersonates gymnastics; it's a dishonest, false, inferior, and vulgar technique that works deceitfully by the help of lines, colors, paint, and clothing, creating a spurious beauty at the expense of the true beauty which is given by gymnastics.

By now, I think you'll be able to follow me. I'd rather not be boring, so I'll use the method of the geometricians to simply say: As cosmetics is to gymnastics, making pastry is to medicine; or as cosmetics is to gymnastics, sophistry is to legislation; and as making pastry is to medicine, rhetoric is to justice.

There is a natural difference between them, but because of their close connection, the sphere and subject of the rhetorician is likely to be confused with that of the sophist. They neither know what to make of themselves, nor do other people know what to make of them. If the body presided over itself and were not guided by the soul, and if the soul did not distinguish between making pastry and medicine, but the body were made the judge and ruled by bodily delight, then the word of Anaxagoras—that word with which you, friend Polus, are so well acquainted—would come true. Chaos would return, and making pastry, health, and medicine would mingle in an indiscernible mass. Now I've told you my notion of rhetoric, which, in relation to the soul, is what making pastry is to the body. I may have been inconsistent in making a long speech, because I wouldn't allow you to speak at length, but I think I should be excused. Because you didn't understand my shorter answer, I had to offer an explanation. If I'm unable to understand yours, I invite you to speak at length. But if I am able to understand you, let me benefit from your brevity; that's only fair. Now this answer of **[466]** mine is at your service.

Polus: What do you mean? Do you think that rhetoric is flattery?

Socrates: No, I said a part of flattery. If you can't remember at your age, Polus, what will you do when you get older?

Polus: And are the good rhetoricians poorly regarded in the state because they are considered to be flatterers?

Socrates: Is that a question or the beginning of a speech?

Polus: I'm asking a question.

Socrates: Then my answer is that they aren't regarded at all.

Polus: What do you mean, not regarded? Don't they have great power in the state?

Socrates: Not if you mean to say that power is something good for the person who has it.

Polus: I do mean to say that.

Socrates: Then, I think that they have the least power of all citizens.

Polus: What! Aren't they like dictators, able to kill, rob, or exile anyone they want?

Socrates: Polus, whenever you speak, I can't figure out whether you are asking me a question or giving your own opinion.

Polus: I'm asking you a question.

Socrates: My friend, you are asking two questions at the same time.

Polus: What do you mean, two questions?

Socrates: Didn't you just say that rhetoricians are like tyrants, able to kill, rob, or exile anyone they want?

Polus: I did.

Socrates: Well, then I think there are two questions in one, and I'll answer both of them. Polus, rhetoricians and dictators have the least possible power in the state, as I just said. The reason is that they don't do what they really want, but only what they believe to be best.

Polus: Isn't that a lot of power?

Socrates: Polus has already denied that.

Polus: Denied? No, that's what I affirm!

Socrates: Not you, because you say that great power is good for the person who has the power.

Polus: Yes, I do.

Socrates: Would you say that if a fool does what appears to be best, then the fool does what's good? Would you call that great power?

Polus: Of course not.

Socrates: Then you must prove that the rhetorician isn't a fool and that rhetoric is an art rather than mere flattery. That's the way to refute me. But if you leave me unrefuted, then **[467]** rhetoricians—and dictators—who do what they think is best in the state will be shown to have no power. You assume that power is a good thing; and yet you admit that power which is used without understanding is evil?

Polus: Yes, I admit that.

Socrates: Then how can rhetoricians or dictators have great power in the state unless Polus can refute Socrates and prove to him that they do what they really want?

Polus: Honestly, this guy . . .

Socrates: I say that they don't do what they really want; now refute me.

Polus: O.K., haven't you admitted that they do what they think is best?

Socrates: I still admit that.

Polus: Then it's clear that they do what they want?

Socrates: To that I say "No."

Polus: And yet they do what they think is best?

Socrates: Sure.

Polus: Socrates, that's absurd—outrageous.

Socrates: Good words, good Polus, if I may use your own peculiar style. But if you wish to question me, either prove that I'm wrong or give a better answer.

Polus: All right, I'm willing to answer your questions so I can understand what you mean.

Socrates: Do you think that people choose to do what they do, or do they choose something else, some larger purpose for the sake of which they do what they do? For example, when they take medicine their physician has prescribed, do they choose the drinking of repulsive medicine or health, which is their real goal?

Polus: Obviously, the health.

Socrates: By the same token, when people take a business trip, they don't choose the traveling. Who would desire the risk of taking a trip or the trouble of doing business? They choose to have the wealth for the sake of which they take the business trip.

Polus: Of course.

Socrates: Isn't this generally true? A person who does something for the sake of something else does not choose the immediate activity but that for the sake of which it is done.

Polus: Yes.

Socrates: Wouldn't you say that everything we choose is either good, bad, or indifferent?

Polus: I suppose so.

Socrates: Wisdom, health, and wealth—wouldn't you call them good and their opposites bad?

Polus: I'd say so.

Socrates: Consider the things which are neither good nor bad in themselves, sometimes **[468]** being good, sometimes being bad, and sometimes being neither. For example, take sitting, walking, running, sailing, wood, stones, etc.; wouldn't you call these neither good nor bad?

Polus: That's right.

Socrates: Are these neutral activities done for the sake of the good, or does the good exist for the sake of what is neutral?

Polus: Clearly, the neutral is done for the sake of the good.

Socrates: When we walk, we walk for the sake of the good, motivated by the idea that the good is better; and when we stand we stand for the sake of the good?

Polus: Yes.

Socrates: And if we should kill or exile someone or take that person's property, we do that because we think it is for our good?

Polus: Certainly.

Socrates: People who do such things do them all for the sake of the good?

Polus: I admit that.

Socrates: Didn't we agree that when we do something for the sake of something else, we don't choose the things we do but the thing for the sake of which we do them?

Polus: True.

Socrates: Then we don't simply choose to kill or to exile a person or to take that person's property, but we choose what contributes to our good, and if the act doesn't contribute to our good we don't choose it. Because, as you say, we choose what is good for us, but we do not choose what is neither good nor evil nor what is simply evil. Why are you silent, Polus? Am I not right?

Polus: Yes, you're right.

Socrates: Given that, if you were a dictator or a rhetorician and killed or exiled someone or stole that person's property, thinking that it is in your interest when it is not, would you say that you do what seems best?

Polus: Yes.

Socrates: But do you do what you choose if you do what's bad? Why don't you answer?

Polus: Well, I suppose not.

Socrates: Then if great power is good, as you claim, would you in that case have great power in the state?

Polus: No.

Socrates: Then I was right in saying you may do what seems good in a state, but not have great power and not do what you choose?

Polus: As if you, Socrates, wouldn't like to have the power to do what seems good to you in **[469]** the state; you wouldn't be jealous when you see a man killing or taking property or imprisoning anyone he pleases. Oh, no!

Socrates: Do you mean justly or unjustly?

Polus: In either case, is such a person not equally to be envied?

Socrates: That's enough, Polus!

Polus: Why is that enough?

Socrates: Because you shouldn't envy miserable people; you should pity them.

Polus: And the people I was talking about are miserable?

Socrates: Yes, certainly they are.

Polus: And so you think that a person who slays anyone he likes, and justly slays him, is pitiable and miserable?

Socrates: No, I don't think that any more than I think he is to be envied.

Polus: Weren't you just saying that he is miserable?

Socrates: Yes, my friend, if he killed someone unjustly. In that case he is also to be pitied. But he is not to be envied if he killed unjustly.

Polus: At any rate you will agree that a person who is unjustly put to death is miserable and to be pitied?

Socrates: Not as much, Polus, as the one who kills him, and not as much as the one who is justly killed.

Polus: How can that be, Socrates?

Socrates: Because doing injustice is the greatest of evils.

Polus: Is that the greatest? Isn't suffering injustice a greater evil?

Socrates: Certainly not.

Polus: Then would you rather suffer than do injustice?

Socrates: I wouldn't like either, but if I have to choose between them, I'd rather suffer than do.

Polus: Then you wouldn't like to be a dictator?

Socrates: Not if you mean what I mean by that term.

Polus: As I said before, I mean the power to do in the state whatever seems good to you, killing, banishing, always doing what you like.

Socrates: Listen to me, my friend, and then say what you can against me. Suppose I go into a crowded marketplace armed with a dagger. Polus, I say to you, I have just acquired rare power and become a dictator, because if I think that any of these people you see ought to be put to death, that person is as good as dead. If I'd like to bash in the head or rip the clothing of that person, that will happen. This is the great power I have in this city. And if you don't believe me, I'll show you the dagger. You would probably say: Socrates, in that way anyone may have great power, burning any house, any dock, or any ship in Athens, whether public or private. But this mere doing as you think best is not great power. What do you say?

Polus: Certainly not, when you put it that way.

Socrates: Can you tell me what's wrong with such power? **[470]**

Polus: I can.

Socrates: Then what?

Polus: What? A person who did what you said would certainly be punished.

Socrates: Is being punished bad?

Polus: Certainly.

Socrates: Once again, my friend, would you agree that great power is good for you if your actions work to your advantage, and that this is the meaning of great power? But if not, then power is bad; it's no power at all. Let's look at it another way. Do you think that the things we were talking about—killing, exile, and taking property—are sometimes good and sometimes not good?

Polus: Certainly.

Socrates: We agree about that?

Polus: Yes.

Socrates: Now tell me when you say they are good and when they are bad. How do you determine that?

Polus: Socrates, I'd rather have you answer that.

Socrates: Well, Polus, since you'd rather have me answer, I'd say that they are good when they are just and bad when they are unjust.

Polus: Though you are hard to refute, Socrates, a child could disprove that statement.

Socrates: Then I'd be grateful to the child, and equally grateful to you if you will deliver me from my foolishness. I hope you will not grow tired of helping a friend but will refute me.

Polus: Socrates, I need not go far or appeal to antiquity. Yesterday's events are enough to refute you and prove that many unjust people are happy.

Socrates: What events?

Polus: I assume you know that Archelaus, the son of Perdiccas, is now the ruler of Macedonia.

Socrates: I have heard that.

Polus: Do you think that he's happy or miserable?

Socrates: I can't say, Polus, for I've never met him.

Polus: Can't you tell immediately, without having met him, whether a man is happy?

Socrates: I cannot.

Polus: Then I suppose you would say that you don't even know whether the Great King[2] is happy.

Socrates: That's true, because I don't know how he stands in relation to education and justice.

Polus: What? You think that's all there is to happiness?

Socrates: Yes, Polus, that's what I think. Men and women who are gentle and good are also happy, and the unjust and evil are miserable.

Polus: Then, according to you, Archelaus is miserable? **[471]**

Socrates: Yes, my friend, if he's unjust.

Polus: I can't deny that he's unjust. He had no claim to the throne that he now occupies; he was the only son of a woman who was the slave of Alcetas, the brother of Perdiccas. Strictly speaking, he was the slave of Alcetas himself. According to your view, if he had been just he would have remained a slave and would have been happy. But now he is extremely miserable, because he is guilty of the greatest crimes. In the first place, he invited his uncle and master, Alcetas, to come to him, pretending that he would restore him to the throne which Perdiccas had usurped. He entertained him and his son Alexander, who was his own cousin and nearly his same age. He got them drunk, threw them into a wagon, carried them off at night, and murdered them. That's how he got them out of the way. After having done all this injustice, he never discovered that he was the most miserable of men. So far was he from repenting, I'll tell you how he showed his remorse. He had a younger brother who was seven years old, the legitimate son of Perdiccas, the heir to whom the kingdom rightly belonged. Archelaus had no mind to be happy by bringing him up as he should and restoring the kingdom to him. He drowned him by throwing him into a well. Then he told his mother, Cleopatra, that he had fallen in while running after a goose. Because he is the greatest criminal in all Macedonia, I suppose he is the most miserable and not the happiest. Surely his misery would not be desired by any Athenian, least of all by you. He is the last Macedonian with whom you would trade places.

Socrates: I described you at first, Polus, as being a rhetorician rather than a person skilled in reasoning. Now I suppose this is the sort of argument with which, you imagine, a child might refute me and by which I stand refuted when I say that the unjust man is not happy. But my friend, where is the refutation? I don't admit a word you've been saying.

Polus: That's only because you don't want to; surely you think as I do. **[472]**

Socrates: Not so, my friend. The problem is that you are trying to refute me with rhetoric, the way they do in law courts. There the one side thinks that they refute the other when they bring in a number of witnesses with a good reputation to prove their allegations, whereas their adversary has only a single one or none at all. But this kind of proof is worthless when we are concerned with the truth. Sometimes a person may be slandered by a crowd of false witnesses. I know that nearly everyone, whether an Athenian or a stranger, will be on your side in this argument. If you want to bring witnesses in to disprove my position, you may summon Nicias, the son of Niceratus, and let his brother, who donated the row of tripods that stand in the temple of Dionysus, come with him. Or you may summon Aristocrates, the son of Scellius, who gave that famous offering that is at Delphi. Summon, if you want, the entire house of Pericles, or any other great Athenian family you choose. They will all agree with you. Only I am left alone in being unable to agree, because you have not convinced me. You merely produce many false witnesses against me, hoping to deprive me of my inheritance: the truth. But I will have proved nothing unless I make you the one willing witness for my position. Nor will you have proved anything unless you have me as the one witness on your side, regardless of the rest of the world. There are two ways of refutation, one which is yours, along with the rest of the world; but mine is of another kind. Let's compare them and see how they differ.   Indeed, the matters at issue are not trivial—knowing or not knowing what makes us happy or miserable. What knowledge can be more valuable than this, or what ignorance more disgraceful? Therefore, I'll begin by asking you about this issue. Seeing that you think Archelaus is unjust and yet happy, I assume you think that a person who is unjust and does injustice can be happy. Am I right?

Polus: Quite right.

Socrates: And I say that it's impossible for him to be unjust and happy. Fine. Do you also mean to say that if unjust people are caught and punished they will continue to be happy?

Polus: Of course not. In that case they will surely be miserable.

Socrates: On the other hand, if unjust people are not punished, then you think they will be happy.

Polus: Yes.

Socrates: But in my opinion, Polus, unjust people, or those who act unjustly, are miserable in any case; but they are more miserable if they are not caught and punished. They are less miserable if they are caught and punished.

Polus: Socrates, you are trying to defend a paradox. **[473]**

Socrates: I'll try to make you agree with me, my friend.   I do regard you as a friend. Here are the points of divergence between us: I say that to do injustice is worse than to suffer injustice.

Polus: Exactly.

Socrates: And you say the opposite?

Polus: Yes.

Socrates: I also say that the unjust are miserable, and you deny this.

Polus: Yes, I did, make no mistake about that.

Socrates: But that was only your opinion, Polus.

Polus: Yes, and I'm surely right.

Socrates: And you said that someone who does wrong is happy if not caught and punished.

Polus: Certainly.

Socrates: And I say that such a person is most miserable and that those who are caught and punished are less miserable. Are you going to refute that too?

Polus: Socrates, that's harder to refute than the other one.

Socrates: Not hard, Polus, impossible. You can never refute the truth.

Polus: What do you mean? If a man is caught in an unjust attempt to become a dictator and is racked, castrated, has his eyes burned out, and after having all sorts of horrible injuries inflicted on him, sees his wife and children suffer, and then is impaled, tarred, and burned, he will be happier than if he escapes and becomes a dictator and continues for the rest of his life doing as he pleases while holding the reins of government and has the envy of both citizens and strangers. Is that the paradox which you say cannot be refuted?

Socrates: You are trying to frighten me with hobgoblins, Polus, instead of refuting me, just as earlier you were calling witnesses against me. But please refresh my memory. Did you say "in an unjust attempt to become a dictator"?

Polus: Yes, I did.

Socrates: Then I say that neither of them will be happier than the other, neither the one who unjustly acquires a dictatorship nor the one who suffers in the attempt, because of two miserable people one cannot be happier. But the one who escapes and becomes a dictator is the more miserable of the two. You laugh, Polus? Well, this is a new kind of refutation. When someone says something, instead of disproving it, you laugh.

Polus: Socrates, don't you think that you have been sufficiently refuted when you say something that no human being will accept? Ask our friends here!

Socrates: Polus, I'm not a politician. Just last year, when the lottery selected me to serve in the Council, I had to take a vote. They laughed at me because I was unable to do it. **[474]** Just as I failed then, you should not ask me to take a vote among the people assembled here. But, as I was saying, if you have no better argument than numbers, let me take a turn and you can judge the kind of proof which I think ought to be given. I shall produce only one witness of the truth of what I am saying—the person with whom I am arguing. I know how to take that person's vote, but I have nothing to do with the crowd and simply do not address myself to them. May I ask whether you will answer my questions and have your own words judged? I think that you and I and every other person really think that to do an injustice is a greater evil than to suffer it. Not to be caught and punished is worse than being caught and punished.

Polus: And I say that neither I nor any other person believes this. For example, would you rather suffer than do injustice?

Socrates: Yes, and so would you. Anyone would.

Polus: No, just the opposite. Not you, not I, not anyone else.

Socrates: Will you answer my questions?

Polus: Certainly. I can't wait to hear what you're going to say!

Socrates: Answer, then, and you'll know. Let's begin at the beginning. Which of the two, Polus, is worse, to do injustice or to suffer it?

Polus: I say that suffering is worse.

Socrates: Which is the greater disgrace? Answer!

Polus: To do.

Socrates: And the greater disgrace is the greater evil?

Polus: Certainly not!

Socrates: Then what do you say to this? When you speak of fine or beautiful things, such as bodies, colors, forms, sounds, or institutions, don't you call them beautiful in reference to some standard? Bodies, for example, are beautiful either to the degree that they are useful or to the extent that they give pleasure to an observer. Can you give any other account of personal beauty?

Polus: I can't.

Socrates: And would you speak of other things—of forms or colors, for example—as beautiful either because of the pleasure they give or because of their use or both?

Polus: Yes, I would.

Socrates: And you would call sounds and music beautiful for the same reason?

Polus: I would.

Socrates: Also, laws and institutions have beauty or excellence only so far as they are pleasant or useful or both?

Polus: That's right.

Socrates: And couldn't we say the same about the beauty of knowledge? **[475]**

Polus: Yes. I approve of your measuring beauty by the standard of pleasure and utility.

Socrates: And by the same reasoning, deformity or disgrace may be measured by the opposite standard, of pain and evil.

Polus: Certainly.

Socrates: So, when comparing two beautiful things one exceeds the other in beauty, the difference is to be measured either by pleasure or goodness or both?

Polus: True.

Socrates: And of two deformed things, the one which exceeds in ugliness or disgrace is either more painful or more evil, doesn't that follow?

Polus: Yes.

Socrates: What was the observation you made just now about doing and suffering wrong? Didn't you say that suffering wrong was more evil and doing wrong was more disgraceful?

Polus: I did say that.

Socrates: Then, if doing wrong is more disgraceful than suffering, the more disgraceful must be more painful. It must exceed in pain or in evil or both. Doesn't that follow?

Polus: Of course.

Socrates: First, let's consider whether doing injustice exceeds suffering injustice in pain. Do the injurers suffer more than the injured?

Polus: No, Socrates, certainly not.

Socrates: Then the injurers do not exceed in pain.

Polus: No.

Socrates: But if they do not exceed in pain, they do not exceed in both pain and evil.

Polus: Of course not.

Socrates: Then they can only exceed in the other?

Polus: Yes.

Socrates: In evil.

Polus: True.

Socrates: Then doing injustice, because it exceeds in evil, will be a greater evil than suffering injustice?

Polus: Clearly.

Socrates: But you and the rest of the world have already agreed that to do injustice is more disgraceful than to suffer injustice.

Polus: Yes.

Socrates: And now it is discovered to be more evil.

Polus: True.

Socrates: Would you prefer a greater evil or disgrace to a lesser one? Answer, Polus. Don't be afraid. You will suffer no harm if you bravely submit to the healing power of the argument, which is a kind of physician. Either say "yes" or "no" to me.

Polus: I would not prefer a greater evil or disgrace to a lesser one.

Socrates: Would any other person?

Polus: Not according to this way of putting the matter, Socrates.

Socrates: Then I was right, Polus, when I said that neither you nor I nor any other person would rather do than suffer injustice, because to do injustice is the greater evil of the two.

Polus: That's true.

Socrates: Then you see, Polus, that when you compare the two kinds of refutation they are quite unlike. All people, with the exception of myself, agree with you. But your agreement **[476]** is enough for me, and I don't need any other witness. I count only your vote, and I don't care about the rest. Well, enough of this. Let's get on to the next question, whether the greater evil for a guilty person is to suffer punishment, as you said, or whether to escape punishment is not a greater evil, as I said. Let's look at the matter this way. Wouldn't you say that to suffer punishment is another name for being justly corrected?

Polus: I would.

Socrates: Would you agree that all just things are honorable as far as they are just? Think about that and tell me your opinion.

Polus: Yes, Socrates, I think they are.

Socrates: Then consider another point. Where there is an agent, must there not also be a patient?

Polus: I admit that.

Socrates: Won't the patient suffer from what the agent does, and won't the suffering have the quality of the action? For example, if a person strikes, there must be something which is struck.

Polus: Yes.

Socrates: And if the striker strikes violently or quickly, that which is struck will be struck violently or quickly?

Polus: True.

Socrates: So, the suffering to one who is stricken is of the same nature as the act of the one who strikes?

Polus: Yes.

Socrates: And if someone burns, there is something which is burned.

Polus: Certainly.

Socrates: And if he burns excessively or painfully, the thing burned will be burned in the same way.

Polus: True.

Socrates: And if someone cuts, the same argument will hold; there will be something cut.

Polus: Yes.

Socrates: And if the cutting is large or deep or painful, the cut will be of the same nature?

Polus: Evidently.

Socrates: Then you would agree to the general statement I was just formulating: What the patient undergoes corresponds to the act of the agent.

Polus: I accept that.

Socrates: O.K. Then tell me whether being punished is suffering or acting.

Polus: Suffering, Socrates. We can't doubt that.

Socrates: And suffering implies an agent?

Polus: Certainly. The agent is the one who punishes.

Socrates: And one who punishes rightly, punishes justly?

Polus: Yes.

Socrates: And therefore acts justly?

Polus: Justly.

Socrates: Then someone who is punished suffers justly?

Polus: That's evident.

Socrates: We agree that what is just is honorable?

Polus: Certainly.

Socrates: Then the punisher does what is honorable, and the punished undergoes what is honorable?

Polus: True.

Socrates: If it is honorable, then it is good, because the honorable is either pleasant or useful. **[477]**

Polus: Yes.

Socrates: Then someone who is punished undergoes what is good.

Polus: That's true.

Socrates: Then that person is benefited.

Polus: Yes.

Socrates: Do you mean what I mean by the term "benefited"? I mean that the person's soul or mind is improved.

Polus: I mean the same.

Socrates: Then someone who is punished is freed from something bad in the soul or mind?

Polus: Yes.

Socrates: Isn't that person freed from the greatest evil? Look at it this way. In economic matters, is there any greater evil than poverty?

Polus: There's no greater evil.

Socrates: In matters of health, you would say that weakness and disease and deformity are bad?

Polus: I would.

Socrates: Similarly, the soul or mind has its own evil?

Polus: Of course.

Socrates: And we would call it injustice, ignorance, and cowardice.

Polus: I agree.

Socrates: So, in mind, body, and economics, which are three in number, you have pointed out three corresponding evils: injustice, disease, and poverty.

Polus: True.

Socrates: Which of these evils is the most disgraceful? Isn't the most disgraceful one injustice, and, in general, the evil of the mind or soul?

Polus: The most evil by far.

Socrates: If it is the most disgraceful, then it's the worst.

Polus: How so, Socrates? I don't understand.

Socrates: We have already admitted that what is most disgraceful is the most painful or harmful or both.

Polus: O.K.

Socrates: So, we agree that injustice and other evils of the soul or mind are the most disgraceful.

Polus: We agree.

Socrates: It is most disgraceful either because it is most painful—causes excessive pain—or most harmful or both.

Polus: Yes.

Socrates: Therefore, to be unjust, uncontrolled, cowardly, and ignorant is more painful than to be poor and sick?

Polus: No, Socrates, I don't think that follows from what we said.

Socrates: Then if it is not more painful, the evil of the soul or mind must be the most disgraceful of all evils. The excessive disgrace must be caused by some excessive harm.

Polus: Clearly.

Socrates: And do you agree that what exceeds most in harm is the greatest of evils?

Polus: Yes.

Socrates: Then injustice and excess and, in general, vice or defect of the mind or soul is the greatest of evils.

Polus: I agree.

Socrates: Tell me, then, what art delivers us from poverty? Isn't it the art of making money?

Polus: Yes.

Socrates: And what art frees us from disease? Isn't it the art of medicine?

Polus: Certainly.

Socrates: And which art releases us from vice and injustice? If you can't answer right away, **[478]** ask yourself where we take the sick.

Polus: To physicians, Socrates.

Socrates: To whom do we take the unjust and uncontrolled?

Polus: Do you mean to judges?

Socrates: To be punished?

Polus: Yes.

Socrates: If they are rightly punished, aren't they punished according to the idea of justice?

Polus: Evidently.

Socrates: Then the art of making money frees a person from poverty; medicine from disease; and justice from excess and injustice?

Polus: That's clear.

Socrates: Which of these three is best?

Polus: What are the choices?

Socrates: Making money, medicine, and justice?

Polus: Socrates, justice is best by far.

Socrates: And if justice is the best, it gives the greatest pleasure or the greatest advantage or both.

Polus: Yes.

Socrates: Is being treated by a physician something pleasant? Does it give pleasure?

Polus: I think not.

Socrates: Then is it useful?

Polus: Yes.

Socrates: Sure, because it relieves us from great evil. This is the advantage of enduring the pain; you get well.

Polus: Certainly.

Socrates: Would a person be more happy concerning health never being sick or being cured?

Polus: Never being sick.

Socrates: Yes, because happiness consists not in being freed from evils but in never knowing them.

Polus: True.

Socrates: Now consider the cases of two people who have some disease. One of them is healed and freed from the disease, and the other is not healed and retains the disease. Which of them is more miserable?

Polus: Obviously the one who is not healed.

Socrates: Didn't we agree that punishment delivers a person from the greatest evils, from vice and injustice?

Polus: Yes.

Socrates: Justice punishes us, making us more just, and thus heals our vice and injustice.

Polus: Yes.

Socrates: So the person who is most happy is the one whose soul has never been corrupted. A deformed and corrupted soul is the greatest of evils.

Polus: Clearly.

Socrates: In second place is the person who has been freed from corruption.

Polus: Correct.

Socrates: This is the person who receives warning and correction and punishment.

Polus: True.

Socrates: And the one who lives the worst life is the individual who is unjust and has not been freed from that injustice.

Polus: I agree.

Socrates: I mean the one who commits the greatest of crimes and, being, the most unjust, **[479]** succeeds in escaping criticism or correction or punishment. For example, you say that is the case with Archelaus, but shouldn't we include all dictators, rhetoricians, and despots?

Polus: I suppose so.

Socrates: My friend, may we not compare their way of operating with the conduct of a person who has a horrible disease and yet refuses to visit the physician to pay for abusing the body? Such a person refuses to be cured, like a child fearing the pain of being cut or burned. Isn't that a parallel case?

Polus: Yes, it really is.

Socrates: Such a person doesn't seem to know the nature of physical health and vigor. Polus, this is clear from our earlier discussion of those who seek to evade justice, which they see only as something painful. They are blind to its advantages. They don't know how much more miserable it is to live with a diseased soul than with a diseased body. I'm talking about a soul which is corrupt, unjust, and profane. They do all they can to avoid being punished and released from the greatest of evils. They provide themselves with money and friends and cultivate to the utmost their powers of persuasion. Polus, if we are right, do you see what follows, or should we summarize the consequences?

Polus: Go ahead.

Socrates: From what we have said it follows that injustice, especially doing injustice, is the greatest of evils.

Polus: That's clear.

Socrates: Being caught and punished provides release from this evil.

Polus: True.

Socrates: Not being caught and punished perpetuates the evil.

Polus: Also true.

Socrates: Doing wrong is second in the scale of evils. Doing wrong and not being caught and punished is first and greatest.

Polus: I agree.

Socrates: Wasn't that the point at dispute between us, my friend? You considered Archelaus happy, because he is a great criminal who has gone unpunished. I, on the contrary, maintained that he and everyone like him who has done wrong and has not been punished is and ought to be the most miserable of people. I also said that the one who does injustice, whether Archelaus or anyone else, is more miserable than the one who suffers injustice. The person who escapes punishment is more miserable than the one who is caught and punished. Isn't that what I said?

Polus: Yes.

Socrates: And that has been proved to be true?

Polus: It has.

Socrates: Polus, if this is true, then what good is rhetoric? If we admit what has just been **[480]** said, then every person ought to guard against doing injustice, because to do injustice is to suffer great evil.

Polus: True.

Socrates: If you, or the people you care for, do something unjust, you ought voluntarily to seek punishment. You should run to a judge as you would to a physician so that the disease of injustice does not become chronic, an incurable cancer in your soul. Must we not conclude that, Polus, given our previous conclusions? Isn't that the only consistent inference?

Polus: Socrates, I can't deny what you say.

Socrates: Then rhetoric is of no good if we use it to help excuse our own injustice or that of our parents, friends, children, or country. Rhetoric may be of use if, instead of excusing ourselves, we accuse ourselves, our family, and our friends whenever we are doing something unjust. Rhetoric is of use if we mean not to conceal but to reveal that injustice so that the unjust may be caught and punished and thus be healed. Rhetoric may be useful if we wish to encourage ourselves and others to stand firm, bravely close our eyes, ignore the pain, and let the physician cut and burn us in the hope of obtaining what is good and excellent. If we deserve flogging, then we should allow ourselves to be beaten; if we deserve confinement, then we should accept that; if we deserve being fined, then we should pay; if we deserve exile, then we should go; if we deserve death, then we should die. We should be the first to accuse ourselves and our own family. This is how we should use rhetoric so that our just actions can be made manifest and we can liberate ourselves from injustice, which is the greatest of evils. Should we admit this or not, Polus?

Polus: Socrates, I think this is really strange, but it seems to be in agreement with your premises.

Socrates: Must we not disprove the premises if we are to avoid this conclusion?

Polus: Yes, we must.

Socrates: Consider the opposite point of view. If I wanted to harm somebody, such as an enemy, then I should use every word and deed to prevent punishment. Let's say that an enemy has injured not me but some third party, then to do maximum harm I should try to prevent a **[481]** trial. If my enemy goes to trial, then I should try to arrange for an escape and help avoid punishment. If my enemy has stolen money, it should be kept or spent rather than returned, ignoring religion and justice. If my enemy has done something worthy of death, it would be best to promote long life, even immortality, for such injustice. These are the uses to which rhetoric should be put, Polus. But rhetoric seems to be of little good to a person who doesn't intend to be unjust. At least we haven't discovered it in our previous discussion.

Callicles: Tell me, Chaerephon, is Socrates serious, or is he joking about this?

Chaerephon: Callicles, I would say that he is quite serious. But go ahead and ask him.

Callicles: By the gods, I will! Tell me, Socrates, are you in earnest or only jesting. If you're serious, and what you say is true, wouldn't that turn human life upside down? It would seem that everything we are now doing is the opposite of what we ought to be doing.

Socrates: Callicles, I'm sure there's a community of feeling among people, even if we experience it differently. I mean, if every individual had private feelings which were not shared by the rest of humanity, I don't see how we could ever communicate with one another. I say this, because I'm aware that you and I have such a common feeling. We are both lovers, and we each have two loves. I love Alcibiades, the son of Cleinias, and philosophy. You love the Athenian Demos, the people of the state, and Demos, the fair son of Pyrilampes. Clever as you are, I have observed that you never dare to contradict any word or opinion of your lover. As he changes, you change; you go backwards and forwards. When the Athenian Demos denies anything you say in the assembly, you adopt his opinion. The same sort of thing happens with Demos, the fair young son of Pyrilampes. You lack the power to resist the words and ideas of your loves. If someone were to express surprise at the strangeness of what you say when under their influence, you would probably reply that you must use the same language as your loves and that this could only stop if they were silenced. **[482]**

My words, like yours, are but an echo. If you want to stop me, you must silence philosophy, who is my love. It is she who is always saying to me what I am now saying to you. She is not capricious like my other love. The son of Cleinias[3] is inconstant, but philosophy is always true. She is the teacher whose words you just heard and about which you are now wondering. You must refute her and show that to do injustice and escape punishment is not the worst of all evils. If you leave her words unrefuted, I swear to you, Callicles, that Callicles will never be at one with himself but throughout his life he will be in a state of discord. My friend, I'd rather have my lyre be out of tune or find that there is no music in a chorus I was directing. I'd rather have the rest of the world opposed to me and contradict me than to be opposed to myself and contradict myself.

Callicles: Socrates, you sound like a real charlatan. You've turned this discussion into a riot. You speak this way because Polus has met the same evil fate that he accused you of bringing upon Gorgias. If I remember correctly, he made that accusation when you asked Gorgias whether, if someone came to him who wanted to learn rhetoric and did not know justice, Gorgias would teach him justice. Gorgias, in his modesty, replied that he would, because people would expect this from him and would be displeased if he declined. As a consequence of his reply, Gorgias was compelled to contradict himself. That delighted you. Then Polus laughed at you—quite rightly, if you ask me. Now Polus himself has experienced the same misfortune. I can't say much for Polus's intelligence when he agreed with you that to do is more dishonorable than to suffer injustice, because this is what led to his being entangled by you. He was too modest to say what he thought, and as a result he had his mouth stopped up. The truth, Socrates, is that you, who pretend to be engaged in the pursuit of truth, are appealing to popular and vulgar notions of value, which are not natural, but only conventional. Custom and nature are generally at odds with each other, so if a man is too **[483]** modest to say what's on his mind, he's compelled to contradict himself.

You are clever enough to use this advantage in winning arguments. When someone speaks according to the rule of custom, you slyly ask a question which is to be referred to the rule of nature. If that person is talking of the rule of nature, you slip away to custom. You did that in this discussion with Polus about doing and suffering injustice. When he referred to the conventionally dishonorable, you pursued his notion of convention from the point of view of nature. By the rule of nature, only that which is the greater evil is disgraceful—for example, to suffer injustice. But by the rule of convention, to do injustice is the more disgraceful. Suffering injustice is not proper to a man but is appropriate for a slave, who would be better off dead than alive; because when wronged and trampled upon, a slave is unable to help anyone. The reason for this is that those who make the laws are the majority of weaklings. They make laws and distribute praise and censure, considering only themselves and their own interests. They terrorize the mightier kind of men, those who would naturally get the better of them, so that they might not get the better of them. They say that dishonesty is shameful and unjust. What they mean by injustice is the desire to have more than their neighbors, because they are well aware of their own inferiority and are only too glad to have equality. This desire to have more than the average person is conventionally said to be shameful and unjust and is called injustice. But nature itself indicates that it is just for the better people to have more than the worse or for the more powerful to have more than the weaker. In many ways nature shows that justice consists in the superior ruling over and having more than the inferior. This is true among human beings, among animals, and, indeed, among cities and races.

On what principle of justice did Xerxes invade Greece, or his father invade the Scythians? I could give numerous other examples. They acted according to nature.] That means according to the laws of nature, not according to the artificial laws that we frame and fashion and use to take the best and strongest of our young people and tame them like young lions, charming them with the sound of the voice, saying that they must be content **[484]** with equality and that this is the honorable and the just. But if there were a man who had sufficient strength, he would shake off, break through, and escape from all this. He would trample under foot all our formulas and spells and charms, as well as our laws which sin against nature. The slave would rise in rebellion and be lord over us, and the light of natural justice would shine forth.

This is the lesson taught by Pindar in the poem which says:

"Law is the king of all, mortals as well as immortals."

This, he says,

"Makes might to be right, and does violence with the exalted hand; as I infer from the deeds of Hercules, for without buying them . . . "

I don't remember the exact words, but the meaning is that he carried off the oxen of Geryon, according to the law of natural right, and that the oxen and other possessions of the weaker and inferior properly belong to the stronger and superior.

Socrates, you would see that this is true if you would leave philosophy and go on to more important things. Philosophy, Socrates, if pursued in moderation and at the proper age, is an elegant accomplishment; but too much philosophy is the ruin of a human life. Even if a man has natural gifts, by continuing philosophy into later life he will be ignorant of all these things which a gentleman and a person of honor ought to know. He will be ignorant of the laws of the state and of the language which ought to be used when men deal with men, whether in public or in private. He will be entirely ignorant of the pleasures and desires of mankind and of human character in general. People of this sort, when they enter into politics or business, are ridiculous, as I imagine politicians to be when they enter the arena of philosophy. As Euripides says:

"Every man shines in that and pursues that and devotes the greatest portion of the day to that in which he most excels."

If he is inferior in anything, he avoids and deprecates that, praising the other from partiality **[485]** to himself and because he thinks that he will thus praise himself.

The right way is to have both. Philosophy, as part of education, is an excellent thing, and there is no disgrace in pursuing such a study when one is young. But, Socrates, when he becomes an older man, then he becomes ridiculous. I feel toward philosophers as I do toward those who lisp and imitate children. When I see a little child, who is not of an age to speak plainly, lisping as he plays, that pleases me. There is an aspect of grace and freedom in his way of speaking, which is natural to his age. But when I hear some small person carefully articulating his words, that offends me. The sound is disagreeable and to my ears has the twang of slavery. And when I hear a man lisping as if he were a child, that appears to me ridiculous, unmanly, and worthy of a flogging. I have the same feeling about students of philosophy. When I see one of your young men studying philosophy, that I consider to be quite in character, becoming a liberally educated man. The man who neglects philosophy I regard as inferior, one who will never aspire to anything great or noble. But if I see him continuing to study philosophy in later life, rather than leaving it behind, I think he ought to be beaten, Socrates, because, as I was saying, such a man, even though he has natural gifts, becomes effeminate. He avoids the real world and the marketplace in which, as the poet says, men become distinguished. He creeps into a corner for the rest of his life and talks in a whisper with three or four admiring youths, but he never speaks out in public like a free man.

Socrates, I feel friendly toward you, much the way Zethus feels toward Amphion in Euripides' play, the one I was just quoting. And I'm inclined to say to you what Zethus said to his brother, that you, Socrates, are careless when you ought to be careful. You have a noble soul, but what stands out is your childish behavior. In a law court you couldn't state your case, **[486]** provide evidence, or prove your point, or testify well on someone else's behalf. You must not be offended, my dear Socrates, for I'm speaking out of good will toward you. Are you not ashamed at being in this condition, one which is to be expected of all who carry the study of philosophy too far? Suppose that someone were to take you or someone like you off to prison, declaring that you had done something wrong when you had done nothing wrong. You must confess that you would not know what to do. There you would stand, giddy and gaping, not having a word to say. When you went to court, even if your accuser were inept and not worth much, if the death penalty were requested, you would die. Socrates, what is the value of an art which converts a sensible man into a fool who is helpless and powerless to save either himself or others when danger is the greatest? Such a person would be robbed of all property and deprived of civil rights, one who could be boxed on the ears with impunity, if I may use such an expression.

Take my advice, my friend, and refute no more. Learn "the arts of business and acquire the reputation of wisdom," leaving these trivial pursuits to others. Whether they are better described as follies or absurdities, they will only give you poverty and an empty house. Stop imitating these petty splitters of words, and emulate only the man of wealth and honor who is well off.

Socrates: Callicles, if my soul were made of gold, wouldn't I rejoice in finding one of those stones with which they test gold, especially if it were one of the best ones? If the use of that stone proved that my soul had been well cultivated, then I'd know that I was in good shape and that no other test was needed.

Callicles: Why do you say that, Socrates?

Socrates: I'll tell you. I think I've found such a touchstone.

Callicles: What is it?

Socrates: I'm sure that if you, Callicles, agree with me in any of the opinions my soul forms, I will at last have found the truth. If a person is to test the goodness or badness of the soul, three qualities are needed: knowledge, good will, and frankness, all of which you possess. **[487]** Many people I've known were unable to conduct the examination, because they were not as wise as you. Others are wise, but they won't tell me the truth, because they lack the interest in me that you have.

These two strangers, Gorgias and Polus, are undoubtedly wise men and my good friends, but they are too modest and not frank enough. Why, their modesty is so great that they are driven to contradict themselves, first one and then the other, in the presence of a large group and on matters of the greatest importance. But you have all the qualities that these others lack, having received an excellent education. Many Athenians can testify to that. And I'm sure that you are my friend. How can I prove that? I'll tell you. I know that you, Callicles, along with Tisander of Aphidnae; Andron, the son of Androtion; and Nausicydes of the deme of Cholarges studied philosophy together. There were four of you, and I once heard you advising each other concerning the extent to which the pursuit should be carried, and I know that the opinion which you formed was that the study should not be pushed too much into detail. You were cautioning each other not to be too wise so that, without your knowing it, this might ruin you. Now, when I hear you giving the same advice to me which you then gave to your most intimate friends, I have sufficient evidence of your good will toward me. The frankness of your nature and your freedom from modesty are attested by you personally, and that is confirmed by your last speech.

Well then, clearly the inference is that if you and I agree in an argument on any point, that point will have been sufficiently tested and will not require any further proof. You will not have been led to agree with me either from lack of knowledge or from excessive modesty. Nor do you have any desire to deceive me, because you are my friend, as you tell me yourself. Therefore, when you and I agree, the result will be the attainment of perfect truth. Surely there can be no more noble inquiry, Callicles, than that for which you rebuke me: What ought to be a person's character; what are the best pursuits; and how far should those pursuits be taken both in youth and in maturity?

Let me assure you about one thing. If I make a mistake in my own conduct, I do not do so intentionally, but from my own ignorance. Therefore, don't refrain from advising me, **[488]** now that you have begun, until I have learned exactly what it is that I should practice and how I can acquire it. If you find me agreeing with your words, and later find that I am not doing that to which I have assented, then call me "dolt" and "worthless," and consider me unworthy of receiving further instruction.

Once again, then, tell me what you and Pindar mean by natural justice. Don't you mean that the superior should take the property of the inferior by force, that the better should rule over the worse, and that the noble should have more than the base? Am I right in my recollection?

Callicles: Yes, that's exactly what I said and what I still say.

Socrates: Do you mean by the better the same as the superior? I couldn't make out what you were saying at the time, whether you meant by the superior the stronger, and that the weaker must obey the stronger. That's what you seemed to imply when you said that great cities attack small ones in accordance with natural right, because they are superior and stronger, indicating that superior and stronger and better are all the same. Or do you mean that the better may also be the inferior and weaker and the superior may be the worse. Or do you mean that better is to be defined the same way as the superior. This is a point I want to have clearly explained. Are the superior and better and stronger the same or different?

Callicles: I'll tell you plainly. They are the same.

Socrates: Then, as you said, the majority is by nature superior to the one against whom they make the laws?

Callicles: Certainly.

Socrates: Then the laws of the majority are the laws of the superior?

Callicles: True.

Socrates: Then they are the laws of the better; for the superior are the better, as you said?

Callicles: Yes.

Socrates: Then the laws which are made by the majority are by nature noble, because they are superior?

Callicles: Yes.

Socrates: Is it not the opinion of the majority, as you also said, that justice is equality and that to do is more disgraceful than to suffer injustice and that equality and not excess is justice? **[489]** Is that so or not? Answer, Callicles, and let no modesty get in your way. I beg you to answer so that if you agree with me I may be strengthened in my judgment by the agreement of such a competent authority.

Callicles: Yes, that's the opinion of the majority.

Socrates: Then not only custom but nature also affirms that to do is more disgraceful than to suffer injustice and that justice is equality. So, you seem to have been wrong in your former claim. And you wrongly accused me when you said that nature and custom are opposed and that I, knowing this, was artfully playing between them, appealing to custom when the argument is about nature and to nature when the argument is about custom.

Callicles: This man never tires of talking nonsense. At your age, Socrates, are you not ashamed to be trying to trap people with words and, when a person stumbles in using a word, thinking that to be a great piece of luck? Do you not see, have I not told you already, that by superior I mean better? Do you imagine me to say that if a mob of slaves and nobodies, who are of no merit except possibly for their physical strength, have a meeting, that their proclamations have the status of laws?

Socrates: So, my philosopher, is that your line?

Callicles: Certainly.

Socrates: Callicles, I suspected that you had in mind something of this sort. That's why I repeated the question about the meaning of "superior." I wanted to know clearly what you meant. I'm sure you don't think that two people are better than one, or that your slaves are better than you because they are stronger. Then please begin again and tell me who are the better if they are not the stronger. Also, may I ask you to be a bit more gentle in your teaching. Otherwise I may have to cut your class.

Callicles: You are ironic, Socrates!

Socrates: No, Callicles, I'm not. I swear by the hero Zethus, in whose person you were just now throwing considerable irony my way. Now, please tell me, whom do you mean by the better?

Callicles: I mean the more excellent.

Socrates: Don't you see that you're simply repeating words and explaining nothing? Will you tell me whether you mean by the better and superior the wiser?

Callicles: Definitely, I do mean the wiser.

Socrates: Then, according to you, one person may often be superior to ten thousand fools. **[490]** That person ought to rule them, and they ought to be the subjects, and the ruler ought to have more than they have. That's what I think you mean, if you agree that one is often superior to ten thousand (and you shouldn't suppose that I'm trying to trap you with words).

Callicles: Yes, that's exactly what I mean, and that's what I consider to be natural justice—that the better and wiser should rule over and have more than the inferior.

Socrates: Stop there. Consider this case. Let's suppose ourselves to be in a group, as we are now. There are a number of us, and together we have a lot of food and drink. There are all sorts of people in our group, having various degrees of strength. One of us, being a physician, is wiser in these matters than the rest, also probably stronger than some and weaker than others. Being wiser, won't the physician be better than we are—superior to us—in determining who should have how much food and drink?

Callicles: Of course.

Socrates: Then, either the physician, being superior, will have a larger share of food and drink, or will distribute it according to superior wisdom and authority. The physician will not personally take a larger share, but will have more than some and less than others. If the physician should happen to be weakest physically, then the best of all will have the smallest share of all. Am I not right, my friend?

Callicles: You are babbling on about food and drink and physicians and other nonsense. That's not what I'm talking about.

Socrates: But do you agree that the wiser is the better?

Callicles: I do.

Socrates: And shouldn't the better have a larger share?

Callicles: Not of food and drink.

Socrates: I understand. Then, perhaps of coats. The most skillful weaver ought to have the largest coat as well as the greatest number of them. Shouldn't the weaver have the best and finest of coats?

Callicles: What is this nonsense about coats?

Socrates: How about shoes? The most skillful and wisest in making shoes should have the best in shoes. Clearly the shoemaker should walk around in the largest shoes and have the most of them!

Callicles: Shoes? Cut it out!

Socrates: Well, if that's not your meaning, perhaps you mean that the wise and good and true farmer should have a larger share of seeds. The best farmer should have as much seed as possible.

Callicles: Socrates, you keep saying the same thing!

Socrates: Yes, Callicles, I keep saying the same thing and talking about the same subjects. **[491]**

Callicles: Yes, and you're always talking about shoemakers and farmers and cooks and physicians, as if they had anything to do with our argument!

Socrates: Why won't you tell me in what way a person must be superior and wiser in order to claim a larger share? Won't you either accept a suggestion or offer one?

Callicles: I have already told you! In the first place, I mean by the superior not shoemakers or cooks but wise politicians who understand the administration of a state, who are not only wise but also courageous and able to carry out their plans, not people who faint from lack of spirit.

Socrates: Most excellent Callicles, notice how different is the charge I bring against you from the one you bring against me. You criticize me for always saying the same thing. But I criticize you for never saying the same about the same things. At one point you defined the better and superior as the stronger. Then you said it is the wiser. Now you present a new notion, declaring that the superior and the better are the more courageous. My good friend, I wish you would tell me once and for all whom you claim to be the better and superior and in what way.

Callicles: I have already told you that I mean those who are wise and courageous in the administration of the state. They are the ones who ought to rule and ought to have an advantage over their subjects. That is justice.

Socrates: Do you mean that they should have more than themselves?

Callicles: I don't understand.

Socrates: I'm talking about self-rule. But perhaps you don't think that each of us must rule over ourselves. Perhaps you think that it is enough simply to rule over others.

Callicles: What do you mean by "rule over ourselves"?

Socrates: Nothing complicated. I mean what is commonly said, that we should be moderate, be in control of ourselves, and should rule over our own pleasures and passions.

Callicles: How charming! You mean to equate the moderate and the foolish?

Socrates: Of course. Anyone can see that's what I mean.

Callicles: That is what you mean, Socrates. Moderate people are fools! How can a person be happy who is the servant of anyone or any thing? On the contrary, I claim that the person who wants to live fully ought to encourage unlimited desire and not curb it. When desire has grown to its fullest, we should have the courage and the intelligence to gratify it and satisfy all **[492]** longing. This is what I mean by natural justice and nobility. But the majority cannot achieve this goal. Therefore, they blame the ones who can, being ashamed of their own inability, which they try to hide. This leads them to say that excess is something shameful. As I said before, they enslave the nobler natures, and, being unable to satisfy their own pleasures, they praise moderation and justice because they are cowards. If a man had originally been the son of a king, or had a nature capable of acquiring an empire or a dictatorship or exclusive power, what could be more shameful or evil than moderation? I ask you, what could be worse for such a man, who could be enjoying good with nobody to hinder him, yet who accepts custom and reason and the opinion of others to master him? Must he not be in a miserable condition whom the reputation of justice and moderation prevents from giving more to his friends than to his enemies, even though he is the ruler of the city? No, Socrates, the truth is this (and you profess to be devoted to the truth): luxury, excess, and license, if they are properly supported, are happiness and virtue. Everything else is custom contrary to nature, worthless human invention.

Socrates: Callicles, your way of approaching the argument shows a kind of noble freedom. What you say is what others think but are unwilling to express. I beg you not to relax your efforts so that we may know the proper guide for human life. Tell me, then, don't you say that for a properly developed person the passions ought not to be controlled, but that we should let them grow to the utmost and satisfy them in some way, and that this is virtue?

Callicles: Yes, that's what I say.

Socrates: Then those who have no wants cannot be described as happy?

Callicles: Correct, because then stones and dead people would be the most happy.

Socrates: Your words remind us of a frightening vision of life. Euripides was probably right in asking:

"Who knows if life be not death and death life?"

Perhaps we are now dead, as I once heard from one of our wise men. He said that our body is a tomb, and that the aspect of our soul in which our desires are located is liable to being **[493]** easily influenced and pulled in different directions. Some clever Sicilian, or possibly an Italian punster, made up a story. He called the soul a jug, because it holds spirits. Ignorant people he called untrained or leaky. The aspect of the soul of the untrained where the desires are located is the uncontrolled and incontinent aspect, which he compared to a jug full of holes; it can never be satisfied. He doesn't think as you do, Callicles, because he claims that of all the souls in Hades these untrained or leaky people are the most miserable. They are busy carrying water in a sieve to a jug which is full of holes. The sieve he compares to the soul of ignorant people, which is full of holes and therefore incontinent, due to their poor memory. I realize that this story is a bit strange, but it does show what I hope to prove. You should change your mind and, instead of an uncontrolled and unsatisfied life, you should choose one which is orderly and satisfied when its basic needs are met. Does this make any impression on you? Are you coming around to the view that the orderly are happier than the uncontrolled? Or have I failed to persuade you? Will you continue to hold the same opinion, no matter how many such stories I tell?

Callicles: The latter is more like the truth, Socrates.

Socrates: Well, here's another image which comes from the same school. Consider this as an account of the different lives of the moderate and the uncontrolled. There are two men, each with a number of barrels. One man's barrels are sound and filled, one with wine, another with honey, and a third with milk. There are several others, filled with various other liquids. A few thin streams which fill them are hard to obtain and can be acquired only with a great deal of work and difficulty. But once they are filled, his work is done. He has no further trouble with them, nor do they need any more attention. The other man can obtain streams to fill his barrels, also only with difficulty. His barrels are unsound and leaky. Day and night he spends his time filling them, and if he stops he experiences terrible pains. Such are their **[494]** respective lives. Now, would you say that the life of the uncontrolled man is happier than that of the moderate? Have I convinced you that the moderate life is better?

Callicles: No, you have not convinced me, Socrates. The one who has filled himself no longer has any pleasure left. As I have already said, this is the life of a stone. He has neither joy nor sorrow after he has once been filled. The life of pleasure is an ever-flowing stream.

Socrates: If a stream is always flowing in, there must be a stream always flowing out; and the holes must be large to allow the discharge?

Callicles: Of course.

Socrates: The condition you are now describing is neither that of a dead person nor of a stone, but of a cormorant, a bird which simultaneously eats and defecates. Your happy person must be constantly hungry and eating?

Callicles: Yes.

Socrates: And always thirsty and drinking?

Callicles: Yes, that is what I mean. The happy person will have all the other desires as well, and will be able to live happily by gratifying them.

Socrates: Great! Excellent! Go on, Callicles, continue as you've begun. Don't be ashamed. I won't be either. First, tell me whether you include itching and scratching in your life of happiness, assuming, of course, that you have ample scratching and can go on scratching throughout your life.

Callicles: That's rubbish, Socrates; you really are a charlatan.

Socrates: Callicles, that's how I brought out the modesty in Polus and Gorgias. But your modesty will not emerge, because you are a brave man and resist such emotions. Now, answer my question.

Callicles: My answer is that the scratcher would live pleasantly.

Socrates: And if pleasantly, then happily?

Callicles: Sure.

Socrates: But what if the itching is not confined to the head? Do I have to pursue the matter? Callicles, I ask you to consider the logical extreme of this question. Think about the life of a catamite [or a nymphomaniac]. Is such a life not terrible, foul, and miserable? Or would you say that they, too, are happy, if they get enough of what they want?

Callicles: Socrates, aren't you ashamed to introduce such topics into the discussion?

Socrates: My friend, am I to blame for that, or the one who says without any qualification that all who feel pleasure are happy, whatever may be the nature of their pleasure, one who makes no distinction between good and bad pleasures? I would still ask you whether you maintain that pleasure and good are the same, or whether there is some pleasure that isn't **[495]** good?

Callicles: For the sake of consistency, I will say that they are the same.

Socrates: You are breaking our original agreement, Callicles. If you say what is contrary to your real opinion, you will no longer be a satisfactory companion in the search for truth.

Callicles: That is exactly what you are doing, Socrates.

Socrates: Then we're both wrong. But, my friend, I'd like you to consider whether pleasure, from whatever source, is the good. If this is true, then the disagreeable consequences which have just emerged are inescapable, along with a host of others.

Callicles: Socrates, that is only your opinion.

Socrates: Do you, Callicles, really hold this view?

Callicles: I do indeed.

Socrates: Then, since you seem to be serious, shall I continue with the argument?

Callicles: By all means.

Socrates: Well, if you're willing to continue, tell me this. I assume there's something you'd call knowledge?

Callicles: There is.

Socrates: And didn't you say that courage implies knowledge?

Callicles: I did.

Socrates: Also, you were speaking of courage and knowledge as different from each other?

Callicles: Of course.

Socrates: And would you say that pleasure and knowledge are the same or not the same?

Callicles: Not the same, Mr. Know-it-all.

Socrates: Would you say that courage differs from pleasure?

Callicles: Certainly.

Socrates: Then let's remember that Callicles of Acharnia says that pleasure and good are the same, but that knowledge and courage are not the same, neither with one another nor with the good.

Callicles: And what does our friend Socrates of Alopece say about this? Does he agree or not?

Socrates: He doesn't agree. Neither will Callicles when he takes a closer look at himself. You will agree, I suppose, that good fortune and bad fortune are opposites?

Callicles: Yes.

Socrates: If they are opposites, like health and disease, they exclude each other. A person can't have them both at the same time or lack them both at the same time?

Callicles: What do you mean?

Socrates: Consider any physical ailment. A person may have the eye disease called ophthalmia?

Callicles: Sure.

Socrates: And those same eyes cannot suffer from ophthalmia and be healthy at the same **[496]** time?

Callicles: No.

Socrates: Once the ophthalmia is cured, does that person also lose health? Do they both go at once?

Callicles: Of course not.

Socrates: That would be absurd.

Callicles: Very.

Socrates: The person takes turns having them and getting rid of them.

Callicles: That's right.

Socrates: And the same is true of strength and weakness?

Callicles: Certainly.

Socrates: And don't good and happiness alternate with their opposites bad and misery in a similar way?

Callicles: Sure they do.

Socrates: So even if there are some things that a person can have simultaneously, good and bad are not among them? Think before you answer, Callicles.

Callicles: I admit that.

Socrates: Let's go back to our former conclusions. Did you say that hunger, I mean the state of being hungry, is pleasant or painful?

Callicles: I said that it is painful, but that eating when you are hungry is pleasant.

Socrates: I know. But the actual hunger is painful, isn't that true?

Callicles: Yes.

Socrates: Thirst is also painful?

Callicles: Yes.

Socrates: Do I need to list more examples, or will you admit that all wants and desires are painful?

Callicles: I agree. Don't give more examples!

Socrates: Fine. Would you agree that to drink, when thirsty, is pleasant?

Callicles: Yes.

Socrates: And the word "thirsty," as you just used it, implies pain?

Callicles: Yes.

Socrates: And "to drink" indicates pleasure, the satisfying of a want?

Callicles: Yes.

Socrates: There is pleasure in drinking?

Callicles: Yes.

Socrates: When you are thirsty?

Callicles: Yes.

Socrates: When in pain?

Callicles: Yes.

Socrates: Do you grasp the inference? When you say that being thirsty, you drink, that means pain and pleasure exist simultaneously. Aren't they simultaneous, and don't they affect at the same time the same aspect of the soul or body? Is that true or not?

Callicles: It's true.

Socrates: You also said that a person can't simultaneously have good and bad fortune. **[497]**

Callicles: Yes, I say that.

Socrates: But a person might simultaneously feel pain and pleasure?

Callicles: That's clear.

Socrates: Then pleasure is not the same as good fortune, or pain the same as evil fortune. Callicles, that means the good is not the same as the pleasant.

Callicles: Socrates, what is the point of all this quibbling?

Socrates: You know the point, Callicles; you only pretend not to know.

Callicles: Well, get on with it, and stop fooling around. Exhibit your wisdom in instructing me.

Socrates: Doesn't a person bring an end to thirst and stop taking pleasure from drinking at the same time?

Callicles: I don't understand what you are saying.

Gorgias: Please answer him, Callicles, at least for our sake. We would like to hear the rest of the argument.

Callicles: O.K. Gorgias, but I resent Socrates' constant trifling. He is always haggling over little and insignificant issues.

Gorgias: What does it matter? That does you no harm, Callicles. Let Socrates argue in his own way.

Callicles: Well, then, Socrates, go ahead and ask your trivial little questions, to humor Gorgias.

Socrates: You are to be envied, Callicles. You have been initiated into the great mysteries before being initiated into the little ones. I didn't think that was allowed. But let's return to our argument. Doesn't a person stop being thirsty and stop feeling pleasure from drinking at the same time?

Callicles: That's true.

Socrates: If you are hungry, or have any other desire, don't you lose the desire and the pleasure at the same moment?

Callicles: True.

Socrates: Then pain and pleasure cease at the same moment?

Callicles: Yes.

Socrates: But good and bad do not cease at the same moment. You admitted that; do you still admit it?

Callicles: Yes, I do. But what is the point?

Socrates: My friend, the point is that the good is not the same as the pleasant, or the bad the same as the painful. Pain and pleasure cease at the same time, but good and bad do not. So, how could pleasure be the same as good or pain be the same as bad? Let's look at the matter from another point of view. I doubt that this occurred to you. Aren't good things good because of the presence of goodness in them, just as beautiful things are those that have beauty present in them?

Callicles: I suppose.

Socrates: And didn't you just deny that fools and cowards are good, whereas courageous and wise people are good? You'd say that, wouldn't you?

Callicles: Certainly I would.

Socrates: And did you ever see a foolish child enjoying pleasure?

Callicles: Yes.

Socrates: And also a foolish adult?

Callicles: Sure, but what is your point?

Socrates: Don't ask; just answer. **[498]**

Callicles: Yes.

Socrates: And did you ever see an intelligent person in a state of joy or sorrow?

Callicles: Of course.

Socrates: Who rejoices and sorrows most, wise people or foolish people?

Callicles: There is not much difference between them.

Socrates: O.K. Did you ever see a coward in battle?

Callicles: I have.

Socrates: Who appeared to rejoice more when the enemy departed, the coward or the brave person?

Callicles: They both rejoiced about equally.

Socrates: So, cowards rejoice?

Callicles: Greatly.

Socrates: Foolish people do as well?

Callicles: Yes.

Socrates: And do only cowards feel pain when the enemy approaches, or are brave people also pained?

Callicles: Both are pained.

Socrates: And are they equally pained?

Callicles: I suppose that cowards are more pained.

Socrates: Are they not better pleased at the departure of the enemy?

Callicles: Sure.

Socrates: Then are the foolish and the wise and the cowards and the brave all nearly equally pleased and pained, as you said, but the cowards more pleased and pained than the brave?

Callicles: Yes.

Socrates: But you think that the wise and brave are good and the foolish and cowardly are bad?

Callicles: I do.

Socrates: Then are the good and the bad nearly equally pleased and pained?

Callicles: Yes.

Socrates: Then are the good and bad equally good and equally bad, or do the bad have the advantage in both good and evil?

Callicles: I don't have the faintest idea what you're talking about!

Socrates: Don't you remember saying that the good are good because goodness is present in them, and bad because of badness? And didn't you also say that pleasures are good and pain bad?

Callicles: Yes. I do remember saying that.

Socrates: And are not these pleasures or goods present to those who rejoice, when they rejoice?

Callicles: Certainly.

Socrates: Then those who rejoice are good by reason of the presence of goodness?

Callicles: Yes.

Socrates: And those who are in pain have badness or sorrow present in them?

Callicles: Yes.

Socrates: And would you say that the bad are bad by reason of the presence of badness, or would you retract that?

Callicles: I would agree with it.

Socrates: Then those who rejoice are good, and those who are in pain are bad?

Callicles: Yes.

Socrates: The degrees of good and bad vary with the degrees of pleasure and pain?

Callicles: Yes.

Socrates: Have the wise person and the fool, the brave and the coward, joy in nearly equal degrees? Or would you say that the coward has more?

Callicles: I would say he has more.

Socrates: Then help me draw the conclusion which follows from our premises, for twice and thrice over, as they say, it is good to repeat and review what is good. Both the wise person and the brave person we say to be good? **[499]**

Callicles: Yes.

Socrates: And the foolish person and the coward are bad?

Callicles: Yes.

Socrates: And the one who has joy is good?

Callicles: Certainly.

Socrates: We say further that good and evil people both feel joy and pain, and perhaps that evil people have more of them.

Callicles: Yes.

Socrates: Then must we not infer that the bad person is as good as the good person, or perhaps even better? Doesn't this conclusion follow logically from the claim that goodness and pleasure are the same? Can this be denied, Callicles?

Callicles: I have been listening to you and making admissions to you, Socrates, and I observe that if anyone makes any concession to you, even in jest, you fasten on it like a child. But do you really think that I or any other human being denies that some pleasures are good and others bad?

Socrates: Ah, Callicles, how unfair you are! You're treating me as if I were a child, sometimes saying one thing and sometimes saying another. Are you trying to deceive me? I thought you were my friend, one who would never deceive me if you could help it. But I guess I was mistaken, so now I must make the best of a bad business, as the saying goes, and take what I can get. Now may I assume that some pleasures are good and others are bad, as I understand you now to mean?

Callicles: Yes.

Socrates: The beneficial pleasures are good and the harmful pleasures are bad?

Callicles: Sure.

Socrates: And the beneficial are the ones that do what is good, and the harmful are the ones that do what is bad?

Callicles: Yes.

Socrates: Let's consider an example. In the case of the bodily pleasures of eating and drinking which we just discussed, do you mean to say that those which promote health, or any other bodily excellence, are good, and their opposites are bad?

Callicles: Of course.

Socrates: Similarly, there are good pains and bad pains?

Callicles: That's right.

Socrates: And we ought to choose and use the good pleasures and pains?

Callicles: Certainly.

Socrates: But not the bad ones?

Callicles: Obviously.

Socrates: Right, because, as you remember, Polus and I agreed that all our actions ought to be done for the sake of the good. Do you agree with us in saying that the good is the goal of all our actions and that all our actions ought to be done for the sake of the good, and not the good for the sake of our actions? Will you add a third vote for that proposition? **[500]**

Callicles: I will.

Socrates: So, pleasure and everything else is for the sake of good, and not good for the sake of pleasure?

Callicles: Sure.

Socrates: Can anyone determine which pleasures are good and which are bad, or does such discrimination require art or knowledge?

Callicles: It requires art.

Socrates: Let me remind you of what I said to Gorgias and Polus. I said that there are some practices which aim at pleasure, and only at pleasure, and which are oblivious to good and bad. There are other practices which require the knowledge of good and bad. I said that making pastry, which I don't consider to be an art but only a kind of experience, is concerned merely with pleasure and is oblivious to good and bad, whereas medicine is an art that is concerned with the good. Now, Callicles, by the god of friendship, I beg you not to jest or to suppose that I'm jesting. Don't give random answers that are not your real opinion, because we are considering how to live the best possible life. What question can be more serious than this one to a person who has any sense at all? Should one follow the way of life you endorse, learning the manly art of speaking in the assembly, cultivating rhetoric, and engaging in public affairs the way you do? Or should one pursue a philosophical life? In order to make that choice, we must know the difference between these two kinds of life. So, let's begin there, as I tried to do earlier. After that, we can agree about whether these two really are different. If they are, we can go on to consider how they differ and, above all, which one we should choose. But it's possible that even now you don't understand what I mean.

Callicles: You are right. I do not understand.

Socrates: Then I'll try to explain more clearly. So far we seem to agree on the following: There is such a thing as good, and there is such a thing as pleasure. Pleasure is not the same as good. Pursuing and acquiring pleasure is different from pursuing and acquiring the good. Do we agree on these points or not?

Callicles: Yes, we agree.

Socrates: Then let's see whether you agree that I spoke the truth when I said to Gorgias and Polus that making pastry is not an art but only a kind of experience. Also when I said that **[501]** medicine is an art that considers the patient's constitution and in each case proceeds according to principles and reasons, whereas making pastry only promotes pleasure, without considering either the nature of the pleasure or the reason for it. It is not an art, because it fails either to examine or deliberate. It operates only by experience and routine which simply memorize the customary means of obtaining pleasure.

First, Callicles, consider whether this has been proved to your satisfaction. Also consider whether or not there are similar practices which have to do with the soul, some of them artistic and deliberative in nature, concerned with the soul's best interest. Are there not others which despise such deliberation and, as in the case of pastry making, consider only how to gratify, never determining which pleasures are good or bad? In my opinion there are other such practices, which I called "flattery." Whether concerned with the body or the soul, flattery is employed only for the sake of pleasure, without considering what is good and bad. Tell me, Callicles, whether you agree with me or not.

Callicles: I agree with you, Socrates, because that's the quickest way to bring this discussion to an end and thus to oblige my friend Gorgias.

Socrates: Does flattery work only on a single individual or on two or more?

Callicles: On two or more.

Socrates: Then it is possible to delight and flatter a whole assembly, with no regard for their true interest?

Callicles: Yes.

Socrates: Can you enumerate the pursuits which delight humankind? Or perhaps you would prefer to have me list some and you can tell me which belong in the category of flattery and which not. What do you say about flute-playing? Doesn't that seem to be an art which only seeks pleasure, Callicles, and thinks of nothing else?

Callicles: It seeks only pleasure.

Socrates: Isn't the same true of all similar arts, such as playing the lyre at festivals?

Callicles: Yes.

Socrates: What about choral performances, especially dithyrambic poetry? Isn't that of the same nature? Do you think that Cinesias, the son of Meles [who composes wildly emotional dithyrambs for the festival of Dionysus], is

concerned with the moral improvement of his **[502]**
listeners or what will give pleasure to the crowd?

Callicles: In the case of Cinesias the answer is clear: He is
only concerned with what will give pleasure to the crowd.

Socrates: What do you say about his father, Meles the harp
player? Did he perform with any concern for the good of his
listeners? Perhaps he wasn't even concerned about their
pleasure when he also inflicted his singing on the audience.
But harp-playing and dithyrambic poetry in general, what
would you say about them? Weren't they invented solely for
the sake of pleasure?

Callicles: That is my notion of them.

Socrates: To what does their solemn sister, the wondrous
Muse of Tragedy, devote herself? Does she aim and desire
only to give pleasure to the spectators, or does she discipline
them, refuse to recite their pleasant vices, and proclaim in
word and song welcome and unwelcome truth? Which is
her character?

Callicles: There is no doubt about that, Socrates. Tragedy
has her face turned toward pleasure and gratification.

Socrates: Callicles, isn't that the sort of thing which we
described as flattery?

Callicles: It is.

Socrates: Now suppose that we strip poetry of melody,
rhythm, and meter. Will speech remain?

Callicles: It will.

Socrates: And this kind of speech is directed toward a crowd
of people?

Callicles: Yes.

Socrates: Then such poetry is a kind of rhetoric.

Callicles: True.

Socrates: So poets who perform in theaters seem to be rhetoricians.

Callicles: Yes.

Socrates: Callicles, we have discovered a kind of rhetoric that is addressed to a crowd of men, women, and children— slave and free. But this isn't really to our taste, because we have found it to have the character of flattery.

Callicles: True.

Socrates: Very good. Now what do you say about the other rhetoric which addresses the Athenian assembly and the assemblies of free people in other states? When they make speeches, do rhetoricians aim at what is best, desiring what will really improve the citizens? Or do they intend only to give them pleasure, forgetting the common good in favor of their own interest, playing with the people as with children, trying to amuse them but never considering whether they are better or worse as a result?

Callicles: I would make a distinction, Socrates. There are some rhetoricians who really do [503] care about the public when they speak, but there are others of the sort you describe.

Socrates: That's good enough for me. Rhetoric, then, is of two kinds, one that is mere flattery and shameful rubbish; and the other that is noble, aiming at the education and improvement of the souls of the citizens. This second kind of rhetoric strives to say what is best, whether welcome or unwelcome to the audience. Callicles, have you ever known such rhetoric? If you have, can you name any rhetorician of this sort?

Callicles: I cannot name anyone among the rhetoricians who are now living.

Socrates: Well, can you identify someone from a former generation who improved the Athenians, someone who found them in a worse state and made them better as a result of making speeches? I confess that I don't know of such a person.

Callicles: What? Have you never heard that Themistocles was such a speaker? Also Cimon, Miltiades, and Pericles, who died only recently, whom you heard personally.

Socrates: Yes, Callicles, they were good men if, as you said at first, true virtue consists only in satisfying our desires and those of others. But if, as we came to realize, that is not so and only the satisfaction of some desires makes us better and some worse, then we ought to gratify only some of our desires. Had any of the men you mentioned mastered the art of distinguishing which are the good desires and which are not? If so, can you identify one of that kind?

Callicles: No, I cannot.

Socrates: Surely, Callicles, you can find such a person if you look. Let's calmly consider whether any of them is of that sort. Won't the good person, who says everything with a view to what is best, speak not at random but according to some standard? Is it not the same in this case as with other artists, whether they are painters, architects, or shipbuilders? Don't they look at the form of their work as a whole, rather than selecting the elements at random?

The artist organizes the parts, forcing each part to harmonize and accord with the others, until **[504]** a regular and systematic whole has been constructed. This is true of all artists. In the same way, the trainers and physicians of whom I spoke before, give order and regularity to the body. Do you deny that?

Callicles: No, I admit that.

Socrates: Then it's fair to say that a house in which order and regularity prevails is good, and one in disorder is bad.

Callicles: Yes.

Socrates: And the same is true of a ship?

Callicles: Yes.

Socrates: And the same may be said of the human body?

Callicles: Yes.

Socrates: Now what would you say of the soul? Will a good soul be one in which disorder prevails, or one in which there is harmony and order?

Callicles: The latter follows from our previous statements.

Socrates: What do we call harmony and order in the body?

Callicles: I suppose you mean health and strength.

Socrates: Yes, I do. And what name would you give to harmony and order in the soul? Can you provide a name for this as well?

Callicles: Why don't you provide the name yourself, Socrates?

Socrates: Well, if you'd rather, I will; then you can say whether you agree with me. If not, you can refute me. Healthy is the name we give to the regular action of the body, and from it comes health and every other bodily excellence. Is that true or not?

Callicles: It's true.

Socrates: And to the regular order and activity of the soul we give the name lawful. The people who make the laws are called lawful and orderly. What is this but moderation and justice? Do you accept that?

Callicles: Yes, I accept.

Socrates: Won't the true rhetorician who is artful and virtuous concentrate on these standards when formulating all words directed to human souls as well as in all actions? Won't this be the aim of the true rhetorician? The goal will be to establish justice in the souls of all citizens and to take away injustice; to establish moderation and take away excess; to establish every virtue and take away every vice. Do you agree with that?

Callicles: Yes, I agree.

Socrates: What good would it be to provide the body of a sick person in a bad state of health with large amounts of the most delightful food or drink? This may be as bad or even worse **[505]** than providing nothing. Isn't that true?

Callicles: I won't deny it.

Socrates: In my opinion, there is no value in a person's life if the body is worthless. In that case life itself is bad. Am I right?

Callicles: Yes.

Socrates: Physicians will generally allow a healthy person to eat when hungry and drink when thirsty, to satisfy whatever desires one likes. But when that person is sick, the physician allows hardly any desires to be satisfied. Do you admit that?

Callicles: Yes.

Socrates: Doesn't the same hold good for the soul? When the soul is in a bad state—is thoughtless, immoderate, unjust, and unholy—then desires ought to be controlled. The soul ought to be prevented from doing anything that works against its own improvement.

Callicles: Yes.

Socrates: It will be for its true interest?

Callicles: Sure.

Socrates: Controlling its desires is correcting it?

Callicles: Yes.

Socrates: Controlling or correcting it is better for the soul than excess and the absence of control, which you previously said you prefer?

Callicles: I don't understand you, Socrates, so I wish you would ask someone who does.

Socrates: Here's a man who can't stand to be improved or corrected as the argument prescribes!

Callicles: I don't give a damn about what you're saying. I have only answered thus far out of courtesy to Gorgias.

Socrates: What shall we do, then? Shall we quit in the middle?

Callicles: That I leave to you to determine.

Socrates: It is said that "a tale should have a head and not break off in the middle." I'd hate to have the argument wandering around without a head. Please go on a little longer and put the head on.

Callicles: You are a tyrant, Socrates! I wish you would either bring an end to this argument, or get someone else to argue with you.

Socrates: But who else is willing? I do want to finish the argument.

Callicles: Why don't you finish the argument by yourself, either by just talking or by question and answer?

Socrates: Must I say with Epicharmus "two men spoke before, but now one shall be enough"? I guess that's how it'll have to be. If this is to be the procedure, I must say at the outset that we should all compete to know what's true and false in this matter, because discovery of the truth is a common good. Now I'll proceed to argue according to my own vision of the matter. If anyone thinks that I arrive at conclusions which are false, you must intervene and refute me, because I don't speak from knowledge of what I'm saying. I'm an [506] inquirer like you, so if any opponent says something cogent, I'll be the first to agree. I'm saying this because I assume the argument ought to be completed. If you disagree, then let's stop and be on our way.

Gorgias: Socrates, I don't think we should leave until you have completed the argument, and I think I speak for the rest of the group. Personally, I would like to hear what else you have to say.

Socrates: Gorgias, I would have liked to continue the argument with Callicles so that I might give him a speech of "Amphion" in return for his "Zethus."[4] But since you, Callicles, refuse to continue, I hope you'll listen, and if I seem to be in error and you refute me, I won't be angry with you as you are with me. On the contrary, I'll inscribe you as the greatest of benefactors on the tablets of my soul.

Callicles: Never mind me, my good friend; get on with it.

Socrates: Then listen as I summarize the arguments. Is the pleasant the same as the good? *No, not the same. Callicles and I have agreed on that.* Is the pleasant to be pursued for the sake of the good, or the good for the sake of the pleasant? *The pleasant is to be pursued for the sake of the good.* Does the presence of the pleasant please us and the presence of the good make us good? *To be sure.* We, and all good things, are good when some virtue is present in them? *That, Callicles, is my belief.* But the virtue of each thing, whether it is the body or the soul, a tool or a living being, best comes about not by chance but as a result of the order, truth, and art manifested in it. Am I not right? *I agree with you.* Doesn't the virtue of each

thing depend upon its order and arrangement? *Yes, it does.*
Is what makes each thing good the proper order it manifests?
That's my view. Isn't the soul which has an order of its own
better than one which has no order of its own? *Certainly.*
And the soul which has order is orderly? *Of course.* And
what is orderly is moderate? *I think so myself.* And the
[507] moderate soul is good? I can give no other answer,
dear Callicles, can you?

Callicles: Go on, Socrates. [Let's bring an end to this farce.]

Socrates: O.K. I'll add that if the moderate soul is the good
soul, the one that is in the opposite condition, the foolish
and excessive, is the bad soul. *True.* Won't the moderate
person do what is appropriate, both in relation to gods and to
human beings? A person isn't moderate who fails to
do what's appropriate. *Yes, of course.* In relationships with
other people, the moderate person will do what is just; and in
relation to the gods will do what is holy. Obviously,
a person who does what is just and holy can't be other than
just and holy. *I couldn't have said that better myself.* The
moderate person must also be courageous, ignoring public
opinion, pleasures, and pains, patiently enduring when it is
right to do so. Callicles, the moderate person, being just,
courageous, and holy, as we have said, is the perfectly good
person. Nor can such a person do otherwise. The person who
lives this way will be blessed and happy, but the bad and
unjust person will be miserable. But this is the person you
applauded, Callicles, the immoderate person who is the
opposite of the moderate. If my view is correct, then I say
that the person who desires to be happy must pursue and
practice moderation and run away from excess as fast as
possible. The best life for such a person is one in which
punishment is never needed. But whenever any of us is in
need of correction, whether a private individual or a whole
city, then justice must be done and the appropriate punish-

ment must be administered. This is the aim a person who seeks to be happy ought to have in living. Individuals as well as states ought to direct all of their energy toward this end, rather than suffering from unrestrained lust and never-ending desire which lead ultimately to a criminal life. Such a person is friend neither of gods nor of human beings, being incapable of community and friendship.

⌜Callicles, philosophers tell us that community, friendship, orderliness, moderation, and justice bind together not only human beings but also heaven and earth. That's why this **[508]** universe is called a *cosmos,* which means order, not immoderate disorder. Clever as you are, you seem not to understand the power of geometrical equality both among gods and human beings. You think that you ought to cultivate inequality and excess and care nothing about geometry. Either you must refute the principle that the happy are made happy by the possession of justice and moderation and that the miserable are made miserable by the possession of vice, or you must accept the consequences of that principle. All of the consequences are true which I stated before, Callicles, when you asked whether I was serious in saying that we ought to accuse ourselves, our children, or our friends when we do something wrong. These are the purposes for which we should use rhetoric. And what you thought Polus was led to admit out of modesty is also true, namely that to do injustice is much worse than to suffer it, because it is more disgraceful. The other position, which Polus thought Gorgias admitted only out of modesty, also turned out to be true: the genuine rhetorician ought to be just and have a knowledge of justice.

Assuming this, let's consider whether you are right in accusing me of being unable to defend myself, my friends, or my relatives when we are in danger. Were you right in saying that I am like someone living outside the human community where anyone might abuse me according to whim, boxing me on the ears, as you put it; or that my property might be stolen; or that I might be banished or killed? You consider such things to be the greatest disgrace. I have given my answer several times, but it won't hurt to say it once more. Callicles, being wrongly boxed on the ears, or even having my face or my purse cut open, is not the worst thing that can happen to a person. Far worse would be to attack and kill me or those close to me unjustly; it would be more disgraceful and more evil. To rob, loot, and enslave, or in any other way wrong me, is far more evil and disgraceful to the one who does the wrong than to the one who suffers it.

These things, which were said earlier in this discussion and which I now repeat, have been fixed and fastened in iron and adamantine bonds. I say this boldly and will continue to [509] do so unless you can break these chains. Until that happens, you can't deny what I say. I don't claim to know the truth about such matters, but I have yet to meet anyone who can say the opposite and avoid looking ridiculous. This has always been my position. If it is true that injustice is the greater evil for the one who does the injustice, or that the greatest evil is to do injustice and not be caught and corrected, then what defense does a person really need? Shouldn't we seek to defend ourselves from the greatest evil? It would seem that the weakest defense is the one which cannot save friends and relatives from the greatest evil. And just as the evils can be graded according to their severity, the degrees of honor in being able to avoid them can be ordered in the opposite way. Isn't that right, Callicles.

Callicles: Yes, that's right.

Socrates: Seeing that there are these two evils, doing injustice and suffering injustice, and because we agree that doing injustice is the greater and suffering injustice is the lesser evil, how can a person acquire a defense which will provide these two advantages, not doing and not suffering injustice? Can power or will provide such a defense? I mean, can a person escape injustice simply by wishing to escape from it? Or is it necessary to have the power to avoid it?

Callicles: It's clear that you must have the power.

Socrates: What do you say about doing injustice? Is the desire to avoid doing injustice sufficient, or is it necessary to acquire the power and the skill to avoid injustice? I'd like to hear your answer to this question, Callicles. Do you think that Polus and I were right in concluding that people do not do wrong voluntarily, but that they do so against their will?

Callicles: I don't want to disagree with you Socrates, because I want to finish this discussion. **[510]**

Socrates: Then it seems that power and skill must be acquired so that we may avoid doing injustice?

Callicles: Sure.

Socrates: What is the art which protects us from suffering injustice? I want to know whether you agree with me. I think that it's the art of the ruler.

Callicles: That's an excellent view, Socrates. See how quick I am to praise you when you make sense?

Socrates: Then what do you think of this idea? It seems to me that we tend to be friends with someone who is most like us—like to like, as the ancient sages say. What do you think of that?

Callicles: I approve.

Socrates: So a rude and uneducated dictator would fear anyone who is superior and would never be able to be really friendly with such a person.

Callicles: That's true.

Socrates: Nor would the dictator be friends with someone who is greatly inferior. A dictator would despise that person and never seek such friendship.

Callicles: That's also true.

Socrates: Then the only friend worth mentioning for a dictator would be someone who has the same character, the same likes and dislikes, yet someone who is also willing to be subject and subservient. That person will have great power in the state; nobody will injure such a person without fear of severe punishment.

Callicles: Yes.

Socrates: If a young person asks how to become great and formidable, the answer is that from childhood on one should feel joy and sorrow on the same occasions as the dictator and be as much like the dictator as possible.

Callicles: Correct.

Socrates: According to you, this is the way to achieve the goal of becoming great and not suffering injury?

Callicles: Exactly.

Socrates: But will this person also escape doing injury? Wouldn't the opposite be true if one is to resemble the dictator in injustice? How else could one gain the dictator's confidence? The young person would have to try to do as much wrong as possible and not **[511]** be punished.

Callicles: True.

Socrates: And so the soul of the young person who acquires power by imitating the dictator will become bad and corrupted. Wouldn't that lead to the greatest evil?

Callicles: Socrates, somehow you always manage to turn everything upside down. Don't you understand that the person who imitates the dictator will kill and take the property of the one who doesn't?

Socrates: Excellent Callicles, I'm not deaf. I've heard that again and again from you and Polus and from almost everyone else in the city. But I wish that you would also hear me. I don't doubt that the person we are describing will kill on a whim; the bad person will kill the good and the true.

Callicles: And isn't that exactly what's so disturbing?

Socrates: No, not to a sensible person, as the argument shows. Do you think that all our efforts should be directed to prolonging life to the utmost and to acquiring whatever arts protect us from danger, such as the art of rhetoric which saves people in courts of law—the art you recommend that I cultivate?

Callicles: Yes, definitely; and I think it's good advice.

Socrates: Well, my friend, what about the art of swimming? Is that a great accomplishment?

Callicles: Of course not.

Socrates: But swimming saves people from death on those occasions when they must know how to swim. If you sneer at swimmers, consider a greater art, that of the pilot. The pilot's art not only saves people's lives but also their physical possessions from extreme danger, just as rhetoric does. But this art is modest and unassuming. It doesn't pretend to do anything extraordinary, but in return for the same salvation which is provided by the one who pleads in court, the pilot asks only a modest fee . . . You know, the pilot is a philosopher, being aware that there is no certainty concerning which of the passengers have benefited and which have suffered by being kept from drowning. The pilot knows that they are just the same when they arrived as when they left, not a bit better either in body or in soul.

This philosophical **[512]** pilot thinks that a person who has some terrible and incurable disease of the body is to be pitied for having escaped and is certainly not served by being kept alive. This would be even more true of one who has a terrible and incurable disease, not of the body but of the soul, which is surely the more valuable part of the person. Such a life is of no value and is not worth having, whether saved from the sea, from the law-courts, or any other devourer. Being unable to live well, the bad person would be better off dead.

This is the reason why the pilot, though our savior, is no more conceited than the engineer, who is equal to the general and the pilot in saving power, sometimes saving whole cities. Is there any comparison between the engineer and the person who pleads in law-courts? And yet, Callicles, an engineer who would take on your grandiose style would have plenty to say; and you would be buried under a mountain of words showing that we all ought to be engine-makers and that engines are the only realities. Nevertheless, you despise a man who is an engineer, sneering at his art and calling him an engine-maker. You would refuse to allow your daughter to marry his son or your son to marry his daughter. Following your principle, what justice or reason is there in this attitude? What right have you to despise the engine-maker and the pilot? I know what you will say: "I am better, being better born." But if the better is not what I say it is, and if virtue consists only in being able to save yourself, your family, and your friends—regardless of your character—then your disdain for the engineer, the physician, and the other arts of salvation, is ridiculous. My friend, I'm trying to show you that the noble and the good might be something different from saving and being saved and that a really good person should not care about living a certain number of years. The good person knows, as we are told, that nobody can escape the day of destiny and should not be excessively fond of life; all that is left to the god. The primary concern should be how to spend your allotted time. You, Callicles, must consider whether the best course is to run your life by the constitution of the city in which you live, becoming as much like the Athenian **[513]** people as possible so that you gain their devotion and acquire power in the state. Please consider whether this is in our true interest. We should be careful about risking what is most valuable to us by acquiring this power, like the enchantresses from Thessaly who, as they say, risk damnation by bringing down the moon from heaven. You are mistaken, Callicles, if you think that anyone could show you the art of becoming a success in the city, whether for better or for worse, without conforming to the ways of the city. In order to deserve being the true natural friend of the Athenian Demos (or of Pyrilampes' dear son who is named after them), you must be like them by nature, and not merely by imitation. Anyone who will make you most like them will make you a statesman and an orator, because we all appreciate being spoken to in our own language and according to our own spirit. But perhaps you think otherwise, Callicles. What do you say?

Callicles: Somehow or other your words, Socrates, always appear to me to be good words. But, like the rest of the world, I'm not quite convinced by you.

Socrates: Callicles, the reason is that the love of the Demos in your soul is hostile to me. But I think that if we return to these same questions and consider them more thoroughly, I may be able to convince you in spite of that. Please remember that there are two ways of instructing, whether we are dealing with the body or the soul. In one we have pleasure as our goal. In the other we seek the highest good, which means we must often resist rather than indulge. Isn't that the distinction we drew?

Callicles: It is.

Socrates: Didn't we also conclude that the one which merely seeks pleasure is just vulgar flattery?

Callicles: I won't disagree.

Socrates: And the other seeks genuine nurture of either the body or the soul?

Callicles: Yes.

Socrates: Shouldn't we have the same goal when dealing with our city and our fellow citizens? Shouldn't we try to make them as good as possible? We've already discovered that it's hopeless to provide them with anything good—not money, public office, or any other kind [514] of power—unless the people who are to have it are themselves good. Shall we say that?

Callicles: If you like.

Socrates: Callicles, if you and I were managing political affairs, advising each other about major public projects, such as building walls, docks, or temples, shouldn't we first consider whether we ourselves know the art of building or where we learned it? Wouldn't that be a good idea, Callicles?

Callicles: It would.

Socrates: Next we should consider whether we have ever constructed any private housing, either our own or for friends, and whether our building was a success. If we discover that we have had good teachers and have been successful in building, not only with their assistance but on our own, then there'd be nothing wrong with proceeding to the construction of public projects. But if we have had no such teachers, have done no building, or have built a lot of bad ones, then it would be ridiculous to undertake public projects or advise each other to take them on. Isn't that true?

Callicles: Of course.

Socrates: Doesn't this also hold in similar cases? If you and I were physicians and were advising each other about our competence to practice medicine, shouldn't we ask each other such questions? How about Socrates himself, is he in good health? Has anyone ever been known to be cured by him? Shouldn't we ask the same about Callicles? And if we arrived at the conclusion that nobody—whether a citizen or a foreigner, a man or a woman—had ever been improved by our medical skill, then, Callicles, how absurd it would be to seek certification to practice medicine. First we must be educated and have gone through an internship. Wouldn't it be foolish, as the saying goes, to learn to be a potter by starting with the most difficult objects, such as a wine-jar?

Callicles: True. **[515]**

Socrates: My friend, you are already a public figure, and you criticize me for not being one, so let's ask each other some questions. Callicles, tell me about making citizens better. Was there ever a person who was vicious, unjust, immoderate, or foolish and, with Callicles' help, became good and noble? Was there ever such a person, whether citizen, foreigner, slave, or free? Tell me, Callicles, if someone were to ask you these questions, what would you say? Whom would you say that you have improved by your conversation? What good actions did you carry out as a private person before you became a public figure? If you have performed such actions, will you list them?

Callicles: You really are belligerent, Socrates.

Socrates: I don't ask this out of belligerence but because I really want to know how you think public affairs should be managed, whether you, as an administrator, have any aim other than the improvement of the citizens. Haven't we already agreed several times that this is the responsibility of a manager? We have surely agreed to that. If you won't answer, I must answer for you. Is this what a good person ought to do for the benefit of the state? Let me remind you of the names we were just now discussing: Pericles, Cimon, Miltiades, and Themistocles. Do you still think that they were good citizens?

Callicles: I do.

Socrates: But if they were good, then clearly each one should have made the citizens better rather than worse.

Callicles: Yes.

Socrates: Therefore, when Pericles first began to speak in the assembly, the Athenians were not as good as when he spoke last.

Callicles: That's likely.

Socrates: No, my friend, "likely" is not the word. If he was a good citizen, the inference is certain.

Callicles: And what difference does that make?

Socrates: None, but next I would like to know whether the Athenians are said to have been made better by Pericles or, on the contrary, to have been corrupted by him. From what I hear it was Pericles who started paying people for fulfilling their responsibilities as citizens and encouraging them to be idle, cowardly, garrulous, and greedy.

Callicles: Socrates, you heard that from Spartan sympathizers, the ones who bruise each other's ears.

Socrates: What I'm going to tell you now is not mere rumor but well known to both of us. At first, Pericles was glorious and his character was unquestioned by any Athenian verdict. That was during the time when they were not so good. Afterwards, when he had made them good and gentle, toward the end of his life they convicted him of theft and almost executed **[516]** him, clearly under the impression that he was a criminal.

Callicles: How does that prove Pericles' badness?

Socrates: Wouldn't you say that a man is a bad manager of horses, asses, or oxen who received them neither biting nor kicking nor butting him and then taught them to do such things? Wouldn't anyone be a bad manager of animals who received them gentle and made them fiercer? What do you say to that?

Callicles: I'll do you the favor of saying "yes."

Socrates: And will you also do me the favor of saying whether humans are animals?

Callicles: Of course they are.

Socrates: Wasn't Pericles a shepherd of people?

Callicles: Yes.

Socrates: If he was a good political shepherd, shouldn't the animals under his care have become more just and not more unjust, as we just said?

Callicles: That's true.

Socrates: Aren't just people gentle, as Homer says? Or do you think otherwise?

Callicles: I agree.

Socrates: And yet he really did make them more savage than when he received them, and their brutality was directed toward him. This was the last thing he would have wanted.

Callicles: Do you want me to agree with you?

Socrates: Yes, if you think I'm telling the truth.

Callicles: I'll accept what you say.

Socrates: If they were more savage, doesn't that mean they were more unjust and inferior?

Callicles: Granted.

Socrates: Then, from this point of view, Pericles was not a good statesman.

Callicles: That is, not from your point of view!

Socrates: No, it's your point of view, Callicles, given what you have just granted. But let's consider Cimon. Didn't the very people he was serving ostracize him so that they might not hear his voice for ten years? And they did the same thing to Themistocles, adding the penalty of exile. They voted that Miltiades, the hero at Marathon, should be thrown into the pit filled with dead people. He was only saved by the president. If they had been really good people, as you say, this would never have happened. Good chariot drivers are not the ones who initially stay in the chariot and wind up being thrown out when they have broken in their horses and have become better drivers. That's not the way it works in driving or any other kind of occupation. Don't you think so?

Callicles: You're right about that.

Socrates: Well, that supports the original claim that nobody has ever been shown to be a good **[517]** statesman in this state. You claimed that this is true of our present leaders but not true of former ones. Now it turns out that they were no better than the present ones. So, if they were rhetoricians, they didn't use either the true art of rhetoric, or the knack of flattery; otherwise they wouldn't have lost favor.

Callicles: Socrates, no living person ever performed as well as any one of them.

Socrates: My dear friend, I'm not attacking them as servants of the state who are able to gratify the desires of the people. They were better at that than those who are living now. But as for transforming those desires and controlling them or using their powers of persuasion and force to improve their fellow citizens—and that's the primary goal of a really good citizen—I don't see that they were a bit better than our current leaders. I admit that they were more skillful in providing ships, walls, docks, and such things.

Callicles, you and I have a ridiculous way of arguing. We keep going round and round the same point and keep misunderstanding each other. Unless I'm mistaken, you have acknowledged more than once that there are two kinds of operations which pertain to the body and two which pertain to the soul. One of them serves our bodies, providing food when we are hungry; drink when we are thirsty; clothing, blankets, and shoes when we are cold; and generally fulfilling their needs. Let me point out that I intentionally use the same images as before so that you may better understand me. The supplier of these things may provide them either wholesale or retail or may manufacture them, being a baker, cook, weaver, shoemaker, or leather-tanner. Such a person is considered by everyone to serve the body.

What they don't seem to realize is that there are also the arts of medicine and physical training which truly serve the body and which should control all other practices through the use of knowledge—such as the good or bad effects on the body of various meats and drinks. The other practices, which are also concerned with the body, lack knowledge and are servile, menial, and short-sighted. Medicine and physical training are the true arts which should manage the others. **[518]**

When I say that this is equally true of the soul, at first you seem to know what I mean and agree with what I say. But a little later you claim that the state has had good and noble citizens. When I ask who they are, you seem to be quite serious when you reply as if you think that Thearion, the baker, Mithaecus, who wrote the Sicilian cookbook, and Sarambus, the vintner, are good physical trainers who excel in their field and serve the body well because the first makes wonderful cakes, the second excellent dishes, and the third wines. They appear to me to be exactly parallel to the statesmen you mentioned. You wouldn't like it if I said that you know nothing of physical training. These people you mention only serve and sell luxury. They have no good or noble ideas of their art but are most likely filling and fattening people's bodies and gaining their praise. But the result is that they lose weight through disease and, in the long run, become thinner than they were when they started.

They, in their ignorance, will not blame their entertainers as the authors of their trouble. After years of excessive eating and drinking, when they are suffering from disease, they will blame their troubles on whoever happens to be near them at the time and offers advice. They might even try to punish that person, but they continue to praise the ones who are really responsible for their horrible condition. That's exactly what you're doing now, Callicles. You praise the men who entertained the citizens and satisfied their desires. People say that they have made the city great, not realizing that the ulcerated and bloated condition of the **[519]** state is to be attributed to these elder statesmen. They have filled the city with harbors and docks and walls and revenues, but they have left no room for justice and moderation. When a crisis brought on by disorder comes about, the people blame the advisors of the hour and applaud Themistocles and Cimon and Pericles, who are the real authors of their calamities. When they lose not only their new acquisitions but their original possessions, if you aren't careful, they may attack you and my friend Alcibiades—not that you are the authors of these calamities of theirs, although you may be accessories after the fact.

From what I can see, and based on what I have been told, there is and has been a lot of foolishness concerning our statesmen. When the state regards any of them as doing something wrong, there is a great uproar and considerable indignation about how badly they are being treated. "After all their valuable service, how could they perish so unjustly?" So the story goes. But this is a lie. No statesman who is really the head of a city could be unjustly put to death by that city. The case of the professed statesman is, I believe, much like that of the professed sophist. Sophists, although they are "wise men," are nevertheless guilty of a strange error. They profess to be teachers of virtue; and then they accuse their students of wronging them, defrauding them of their pay, and showing no gratitude for their services. How could people who have become just and good through the efforts of their teachers act unjustly because of the injustice which they no longer have? Can anything be more irrational than this, my friend? You, Callicles, force me to be an orator, because you won't answer.

Callicles: And you are the man who cannot speak unless there is someone to answer?

Socrates: I suppose I can. I'm making long speeches now, because you refuse to answer me. But I beg you, by the god of friendship, Callicles, tell me whether you see an inconsistency in claiming to have made a person good and then blaming that person for being bad.

Callicles: Yes, I think that there is.

Socrates: Do you ever hear our professors of education saying such things? **[520]**

Callicles: Yes, but why waste words talking about people who are good for nothing?

Socrates: It's better to ask why we are talking about people who profess to be rulers and claim that they are devoted to the improvement of the state and yet frequently complain about how vile the state is. Is there any difference between these two cases? My friend, as I was saying to Polus, the sophist and the rhetorician are the same, or almost the same. But you pretend that rhetoric is something excellent and sophistry something to be despised. The truth is that sophistry is as much superior to rhetoric as legislation is to the practice of law or physical training is to medicine. But isn't it the case that orators and sophists are unique in being unable to find fault with what they give to others, complaining of the harm it does to themselves, without at the same time accusing themselves of having done no good for those they claim to benefit? Isn't that true?

Callicles: I suppose.

Socrates: If they really do make people better, then they would be the only ones who could afford to leave the matter of their pay to those who have benefited from their service. But if people have benefited in any other way—for example if one has been taught running by a physical trainer—payment for that service might not be made. If there was no agreement that the money should be paid as soon as the runner achieved top speed, the trainer should not be surprised at not being paid. People don't act unjustly because they can't run fast.

Callicles: That's true.

Socrates: But someone who removes injustice can be in no danger of being treated unjustly. That person alone can, without risk, leave the payment to the discretion of others, at least if the teacher really has made them good. Am I right?

Callicles: Yes.

Socrates: Then this appears to be the reason why there's nothing wrong with a person receiving pay who is called in to advise about building or any other art.

Callicles: Yes, that seems to be the reason.

Socrates: But if the question is how a person may become truly good and how best to govern both the family and the state, it would be a disgrace to ask for pay?

Callicles: That's right.

Socrates: And clearly the reason is that only such benefits create a desire to repay them. There is evidence that a benefit has been given when the benefactor receives a return, otherwise not. Isn't that so?

Callicles: Yes, that's true.

Socrates: To which service of the state do you invite me? Am I to be a physician to the state who will strive and struggle to make the Athenians as good as possible? **[521]** Or am I to be the servant and the flatterer of the state? Speak out, my friend, freely and fairly as you did at first and ought to do again. Tell me what's on your mind.

Callicles: I say that you should be the servant of the state.

Socrates: The flatterer? Well, that's a noble invitation.

Callicles: Call it by whatever degrading name you want. But if you refuse, the consequences will be . . .

Socrates: Please don't repeat the same old story that anyone who likes will kill me and get my money, because then I'll have to reply that the person who does that is a bad person and is killing a good person and that the money would be of no real use, because what is wrongly taken will be wrongly used. If it is used wrongly, then it is used basely, and if basely then harmfully.

Callicles: How confident you are, Socrates, that you will never suffer such a thing. You seem to think that you live in another world and could never be brought into a court of law. But you are likely to be brought there by some miserable and base person.

Socrates: Then I must really be a fool, Callicles, not to know that in the Athenian state anyone may suffer anything. But if I face the danger you mention, and if I am brought to such a trial, it will be a villain who brings me there. I'm sure of that, because no good person would accuse the innocent. I wouldn't even be surprised if they put me to death. Do you want to hear why I expect that?

Callicles: Of course.

Socrates: I think that I'm one of the few Athenians, perhaps the only one, who practices the true art of politics. I'm the only politician who speaks not with the goal of pleasing but with an eye on what is best rather than what is most pleasant. I'm unwilling to practice those skills you recommend, so I'll have nothing to say in court. The image I used in speaking to Polus might be applied to me. I would be tried just as a physician who had been indicted by a pastry-cook would be tried in a court of children. What would the physician say if someone were to make the accusation this way: "Children, this person has done many evil things to you, especially the youngest among you, cutting and burning and starving you. You have been given the most bitter potions and forced to go without food and drink. How **[522]** different from the wide variety of goodies I have obtained and given to you." How do you suppose the physician could reply in such a predicament? I suppose the physician could tell the truth and say: "I did this for the sake of your health, children." Wouldn't there be a large clamor among such judges? How they would protest!

Callicles: I'm sure you're right.

Socrates: The physician would be utterly at a loss about how to reply.

Callicles: No doubt about it.

Socrates: Well, this is just the sort of thing I would experience if I were brought before the court. I wouldn't be able to review the pleasures I had provided for the people, which they consider to be benefits and advantages, though I don't envy either the ones who provide or the ones who enjoy them. And if it's said that I corrupt the young people and perplex their minds or that I criticize the older ones, whether in public or in private, I would not be permitted to say the truth: That I do all this for the sake of justice and out of a concern for your best interest, my judges, and only that. There's no telling what might happen to me.

Callicles: Socrates, do you think that a man who is unable to defend himself is in a good position?

Socrates: Yes, Callicles, if he has the defense which you have often admitted he should have; if he is able to be his own defense and has never said or done anything wrong, either with respect to gods or human beings. We have often agreed that this is the best kind of defense. If anyone could convict me of being unable to defend myself or others in this way, then I'd blush with shame, whether I was convicted by many people or by few or by myself alone. If I died for lack of this ability, then I would be truly sad. But if I were to die because I lack the power of flattery, the absence of that kind of rhetoric would not cause me to grieve even at the time of my death. Nobody but an utter fool and a coward is afraid of death itself, but we should be afraid of doing wrong. To go to the world below, having a soul which is filled with injustice, is the last and worst of all evils. To prove this, I'd like to tell you a story.

Callicles: All right. You've finished the rest, so you might as well finish this.

Socrates: Then listen, as the story-tellers say, to a pretty tale. I suspect you may be **[523]** inclined to regard it as only a fable, but I believe it to be true. In what I'm about to tell you I mean to speak the truth. Homer tells us how Zeus and Poseidon and Pluto divided the empire which they inherited from their father. In the days of Cronos there was a law concerning the destiny of human beings, one which always existed and still continues in heaven. After death, a person who has lived a life of justice and holiness will go to the islands of the blest and dwell there out of the reach of evil. But a person who has lived an unjust and unholy life will go to a place of vengeance and punishment which is called Tartarus.

In the era of Cronos, and even later during the reign of Zeus, the judgment was given on the very day that people die. The judges and the people were alive, and the result was that the judgments were flawed. Then Pluto and the authorities from the islands of the blest came to Zeus and told him that the souls had wound up in the wrong place. Zeus said: "I'll put a stop to this. The judgments are flawed. The reason is that the people being judged are still alive and thus have their clothes on. There are many who have evil souls adorned by beautiful bodies or wrapped in wealth and rank. When the day of judgment arrives, many people come and testify on their behalf, saying that they lived righteously. The judges are awed by them. They, too, have their clothes on while judging. Their eyes and ears and whole bodies act as a veil before their own souls. All of this gets in the way, the clothes of the judges and the clothes of the judged. What's to be done? I'll tell you. In the first place, I'll take away the foreknowledge of death which they currently have. I've already given that job to Prometheus. In the second place, they'll be entirely stripped before they are judged, because they will be judged when they are dead. The judge will also be naked, that is, dead. As soon as a person dies, the naked soul of the judge will pierce that person's naked soul. The person never knows when death will come, is deprived of kindred, and has left all beautiful attire in the world above. Then the judgment will be just. I knew all about this before you did, so I made my sons judges, two from Asia—Minos and Rhadamanthus—and one from Europe, Aeacus. They will judge in the meadow where three ways meet and out of which two roads lead, one to the islands of the blest and the other to **[524]** Tartarus. Rhadamanthus will judge those who come from Asia and Aeacus those who come from Europe. To Minos I'll give priority, and he'll hold a court of appeal in case the other two are in doubt.   In this way the judgment concerning the last journey of human beings will be as just as possible."

This is a tale, Callicles, which I have heard and believe. From it I draw the following inferences: Death, if I'm right, is a separation of two things, soul and body. It is this and nothing else. After they are separated, they retain their various characteristics which are much the same as in life. The body has the same nature and ways and characteristics, all clearly visible. For example, the person who, by nature or training or both was tall while alive, will remain that way after death. The fat person will remain fat, and someone who had flowing hair will have flowing hair. If a person was marked with the whip and had prints of the scourge or other kinds of wounds when alive, you might see the same in the dead body. If the person's limbs were broken or misshapen when alive, the same appearance would be visible in the dead. In a word, whatever was the habit of the body during life would be distinguishable after death, either perfectly or in great measure and for some time. I also infer that this is equally true of the soul, Callicles. When a person's body is stripped away, all natural or acquired characteristics of the soul are laid open to view. When they come to the judge, as those from Asia come to Rhadamanthus, he places them near him and, not knowing whose soul it is, inspects them quite impartially. Perhaps he may lay hands on the soul of the Great King or of some other king or potentate, one who is unsound, with a soul marked with the whip, full of the prints and scars of perjuries and of wrongs which have been plastered into that soul by each action. Such a soul is all crooked with falsehood and imposture, because it has existed without truth. Rhadamanthus beholds this soul, full of [525] deformity and disproportion, which is caused by license and luxury and insolence and incontinence. He sends it ignominiously to prison where it will undergo the punishment it deserves.

Now the proper goal of punishment should be twofold. One who is properly punished should either become better and profit by it or should become an example to others so that they may see the suffering and thus become better through fear. The ones who are punished by gods and humans and improved are those whose sins are curable. The way of improving them, as in this world, is still through pain and suffering, because there is no other way by which they can be delivered from their evil. But those who have been guilty of the worst crimes and are incurable by reason of their crimes become examples for the others. Because they are incurable, the time has passed when they might receive any benefit for themselves. Others become good when they watch them forever enduring the most terrible and painful and fearful sufferings as the penalty for their sins. There they are, hanging up as examples, in the prison-house of the world below, a spectacle and a warning to all unjust people who come there. Among them, I confidently affirm, will be found Archelaus, if Polus's reports about him are true, and any other dictator like him. Most of these fearful examples, as I believe, are taken from the class of dictators, kings, potentates, and public servants.

Because of their power, they are the authors of the greatest and most unholy crimes. Homer witnesses to the truth of this. Those he described as suffering everlasting punishment in the world below are always kings and potentates. There you will find Tantalus, Sisyphus, and Tityus.[5] But nobody ever described Thersites,[6] or any private person who was a villain, as suffering everlasting punishment because of incurable sin. To do what they did was not in his power, and he was happier than those who had the power. Yes, Callicles, the worst people come from the class of those who have **[526]** power. And yet in that very class there may arise good people, and they are worthy of great admiration, because where there is great power to do wrong, to live and die justly is a hard thing and greatly to be praised because so few attain it in that condition. There have been such good and true people who have fulfilled the trust placed in them, and will exist again in this and other states. There is one who is famous all over Hellas, Aristides, the son of Lysimachus.[7] But in general great people are also bad, my friend.

As I was saying, when Rhadamanthus gets a soul of this kind he knows nothing about it, neither who it is nor who were its parents. He knows only that he has got hold of a villain. Seeing this, the soul is stamped as curable or incurable and is sent off to Tartarus to receive its punishment. Or, again, he looks with admiration on the soul of one who has lived in holiness and truth. This person may or may not have lived a private life, but I would say, Callicles, that such a person was most likely a philosopher who did not trouble with other people's affairs. Such people do their own work during their lifetime. Rhadamanthus sends such souls to the islands of the blest. Aeacus does the same. They both have scepters and judge. Minos is seated, looking on, as Odysseus in Homer declares that he saw him:

"Holding a scepter of gold, and giving laws to the dead."

Now I, Callicles, am persuaded of the truth of these things, and I consider how I shall present my soul whole and undefiled before the judge in that day. Renouncing the honors at which the world aims, I desire only to know the truth, to live as well as I can, and when the time comes, to die. To the utmost of my power, I exhort all other people to do the same. In return for your exhortation of me, I exhort you also to take part in the great combat, which is the combat of your life, greater than every other earthly conflict. I respond to your reproach of me by saying that you will not be able to help yourself when the day of trial and judgment of which I was speaking comes upon you. You will go before the judge, the son of Aegina, and when you are in the hands of justice you will gape and your head will swim **[527]** round, just as mine would in the courts of this world. It is likely that someone will shamefully box you on the ears and pay you every sort of insult.

Perhaps this may appear to you to be only an old wife's tale which you reject. There might be reason in your rejecting such tales if by searching we could find out anything better or truer. But now you see that you and Polus and Gorgias, who are the three wisest of the Greeks of our day, are unable to show that we ought to live a life which does not profit us in another world as well as in this one. Of all that has been said, nothing remains unshaken but the saying that to do injustice is more to be avoided than to suffer injustice and that the reality and not the appearance of virtue is to be followed above all things, both in public and in private life. And when anyone has been wrong in anything, that person should be chastised, because the next best thing to being just is to become just, to be chastised and punished. Also that we should avoid all flattery of ourselves as well as of others, of the few as well as of the many. We should use rhetoric and every other art and perform all our actions with justice in mind.

Follow me, then, and I'll lead you to where you will be happy during life and after death, as your own argument shows. Never mind if someone despises you as a fool and insults you on a whim. Even if that person strikes you, be of good cheer and ignore the insulting blow. If you are really good and true, you will never come to any real harm by practicing virtue. When we have practiced virtue common, we will enter politics, if that seems desir? or we will advise about whatever else might seem go us, because then we will be better able to judge. present condition, we ought not trust ourselves, for ⹁ on the most important subjects we are always changing our minds. What state of education does that indicate? Let us, then, take this discussion as our guide. It signifies to us that the best way to live is to practice justice and every virtue in life and in death. Let's go that way and exhort all other people to follow. Let's not go the way which you trust and where you exhort me to follow. That way, Callicles, is worth nothing.